The Great Divide

The True Story of America Tomorrow

Alan Nevin

A Relatively Unbiased Economist

2nd Edition

ISBN: 153749645X
ISBN 13: 978-1537496450
Library of Congress Control Number: 2016917909

About the Author

Alan Nevin is the Director of Economic and Market Research at Xpera Group. Holding a Master of Arts in Statistics and Research from Stanford University and a Master of Business Administration in Real Estate Economics from American University in Washington D.C., Mr. Nevin has an extensive background in real estate economics, demography, lending and market analysis. He serves the development, investment, legal and public agency communities with residential and commercial real estate valuation, feasibility and real estate advisory services and litigation support.

In the past, Mr. Nevin served as Director of Real Estate Research for HomeFed Bank and was President of ConAm Securities, a subsidiary of ConAm Management Company. Mr. Nevin also served as Chief Economist for the California Building Industry Association.

He is the co-founder of firms that bought, built, rehabbed and operated more than three dozen residential and commercial projects in San Diego County, valued in excess of $250 million. He was a founding member of three savings and loan associations.

Mr. Nevin taught for 30+ years at UCSD Extension. He is an instructor of a CLE-approved seminar on Litigation Economics and taught the capstone course on feasibility studies for the Master's program at USD Burnham Moores Institute of Real Estate.

Mr. Nevin is a past president of the San Diego chapter of Lambda Alpha International, an international honorary land economics society and is a co-founder of the UCSD Economics Roundtable. He also is well known in the business world for his economic and demographic presentations.

The Great Divide

Table of Contents

Introduction

The Great Divide is a book about America and tomorrow. It is a compelling story of **your** future and your children's future as divined through a myriad of research data and my personal travel, teaching, and research.

It is a book about trends, past and future. It is a book that blends demography, economics, and, to some degree, real estate. In fact, I have devoted my professional life to the subjects of both demography and real-estate economics.

This book is not an academic text but rather a highly readable story of changes in our world and our nation. The book relies on facts from the US Census Bureau and numerous other reliable sources. Each of the many tables and graphs tells a story in vivid color.

The trends I discuss herein are real, but they have not usually been widely recognized, because trends happen gently. Most important, trends arc very difficult to reverse. Most of what I discuss here relates to trends that have been going on for more than half a century but are rarely visible to the casual observer. However, these trends will have important and major effects on the economy of our nation and, in many cases, a direct effect on how and where you and your offspring will earn a living.

The book takes a look at the demographic patterns in the industrialized world and compares them to those in the United States. The industrialized world is aging, and that has an enormous effect on the workforce and its ability to replenish itself enough for productivity to be maintained and new jobs to be created.

Within the United States, you will see the remarkable change in the population and employment by region and by state, and you will get a look at the future in terms of where people and jobs are going.

The book divides our nation's metropolitan areas into three categories: the **fast-growing**, the **survivors**, and the **stagnant.** Similarly, the states are evaluated for long-term growth potential. By way of an initial peek at the facts, three-quarters of the gains in population and employment in the nation takes place in fourteen states.

I spend a lot of time talking about California, Florida, and Texas—California because it is more of a state of mind than a state; Florida because it is an integral suburb of New York; and Texas because it is the preeminent symbol of American capitalism and success. The three states together account for one out of every four persons in the nation.

All of these trends have a dynamic effect on the value of your home, your job, and real property. It is inevitable that real-estate values coincide with the paths of population and employment trends.

I don't expect the book to be well received by the dozens of locales I have designated as stagnant or even survivors, as their future is far from rosy. Many of them will go bankrupt because of a declining population, an evacuating young workforce, rising pension obligations, and health and safety budgets. For all intents and purposes, many of them are already bankrupt but not willing to acknowledge it. Most of the stagnant metropolitan areas have pension obligations that are crippling and unforgiving.

Pointedly, the plusses of tomorrow's economies of the world far outweigh the negatives. There are good times ahead for a big part of the world, including, of course, the United States.

I should mention that a brilliant economist Joseph Stiglitz recently released a new book called *The Great Divide* as well. His book is about the great inequality in the United States. My book blends nicely with his, but unlike Dr. Stiglitz, I don't suspect I will get a Nobel Prize..

Without data you're just another person with an opinion.

—W. Edwards Deming

Chapter 1: The World Is a'Changing
Great Surprises Abound

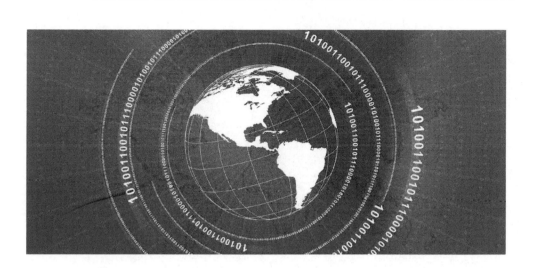

Despite rumors to the contrary, the United States does not operate in a vacuum. I ask you to forget the skirmishes and tribal wars that go on indefinitely in this somewhat disorganized and dysfunctional world and instead look at a bigger picture. It is a picture largely shaped by demographics, which then lead to major changes in the economy and business here and abroad. Many should take heed to Bob Dylan in his song *The Times They Are A-Changin'* for to ignore the demographic shifts one might find themselves sinking like a stone.

Most of the world's business is transacted in a handful of industrialized nations; among them are the countries of the European Union, Japan, China, and the United States. The fifteen largest nations, in terms of gross national income, produce three-quarters of the world's output. The United States, by itself, accounts for almost one-quarter of the world's output.

Gross national income, as shown in figure 1.1, is the sum of value added by all producers in a nation.

Figure 1.1

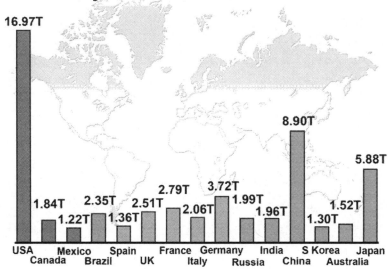

Gross National Income 2013
Major Industrialized Nations

But, dollars aside, the demographics of these nations are changing. The United States is gaining in population at a steady pace, and its population pace far outdistances that of many of the other mature industrialized nations.

Between the censuses of 1980 and 2010, the United States added seventy-eight million people, increasing its base by 34 percent. Comparatively, the other nations noted in the table below have lagged considerably, most adding less than one-tenth of 1 percent annually to their populations. In the 1980–2010 time frame, the five European nations shown here, plus Australia, Russia, Korea, and Japan combined, have not added as much population as the United States.

Figure 1.2

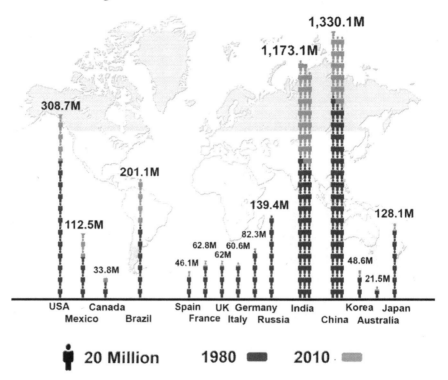

Populations 1980-2010
Major Industrialized Nations

The two most populous nations in the world, India and China, continue to grow, but the growth of their populations, too, is slowing down as their birth rates decline and more of their people move toward the middle class (or, at least, their version of it).

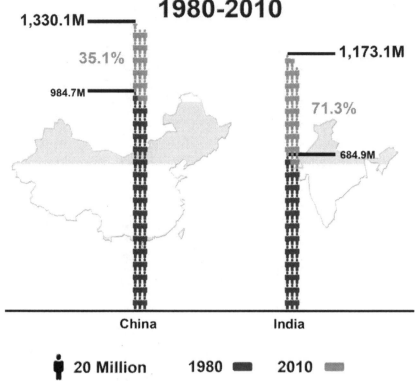

Figure 1.3
China & India Population Change
1980-2010

1,330.1M

35.1%

984.7M

1,173.1M

71.3%

684.9M

China

India

👤 20 Million   1980 ▬   2010 ▬

The growth of China has substantially slowed as a result of its one-child policy. In the 1980–2010 period, India grew by 78 percent while China grew by less than half that amount. Still, the two together add thirty million persons annually to the world population. The United States doesn't add that many in a decade.

In the 2010–2050 period, growth is anticipated to slow dramatically in virtually all the industrialized countries except the United States. We will continue to grow as a result of immigration.

Take a look at figure 1.4 and focus on the population changes in nations like Korea, Russia, Germany, Japan, and China. Their populations are stagnating.

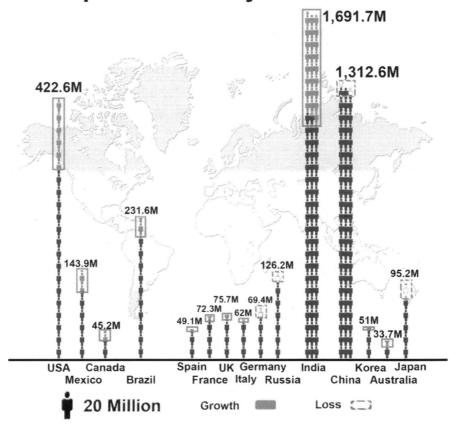

Figure 1.4 **Top 15 Nations**
Population Projections 2050

1,691.7M

1,312.6M

422.6M

231.6M

143.9M

126.2M

95.2M

75.7M 69.4M
72.3M 62M
49.1M

45.2M

51M
33.7M

| USA | Canada | | Spain | UK | Germany | India | | Korea | Japan |
| | Mexico | Brazil | France | Italy | Russia | | China | Australia | |

👤 **20 Million**   Growth ▬   Loss 🔲

Japan, among all the industrialized nations, will experience the greatest decline in population. The decline, 26 percent in a forty-year period, is the result of three factors: xenophobia (the nations near prohibition of newcomers), the exceptionally low birth rate, and the aging of the existing population.

In nations like Japan, the shrinking number of household formations is devastating because it means that there is not a sufficient young workforce to fill the jobs needed to run the country and, secondarily, fewer new households means a declining demand for consumer goods. Therefore, nations like Japan can only survive on providing exports to other nations—but they will not have the workforce to run the factories. While automation shrinks the number of people needed in manufacturing, overall Japan's population trend is not a good situation.

And take particular note of China, which is basically in a nongrowth mode. The one-child policy started three decades ago. The Chinese favor sons over daughters, and, as a result, in the millennial generation (the eighteen-to-thirty-fours), there are substantially more guys than gals (1.4 to 1.0). That means fewer new household formations.

As a result of the demographic pattern, the standard of living will rise in China, and consumer goods will be in strong demand—the antithesis of Japan. However, consumer-goods spending should be much higher in China, but the imbalance between millennial guys and gals makes that impossible.

Here in the United States, we will continue to grow by almost three million people annually, thereby providing a strong market for consumer goods. Consumer goods comprise two-thirds of our economic output, so population growth is imperative for our nation—actually any nation—to continue to prosper.

A similar situation to Japan's exists in Korea, which, according to some sources, will soon become the "oldest" nation in the world.

Many of the nations have an aging population and, typically, that is not good for a nation's economy. As noted earlier, aging nations do not generate a sufficient number of children to satisfy the workforce, but in addition, an aging nation has less productivity and more social and financial burdens on government.

Figure 1.5

Median Age 2010

Major Industrialized Nations

Japan	Germany	Italy	Spain	France
44.9	44.3	43.3	40.2	40

United Kingdom	Canada	Russia	Korea	United States
39.8	39.7	38	37.9	37.1

Australia	China	Brazil	Mexico	India
36.9	34.6	29	25.9	25.5

Japan and most of the European Union are the poster children for aging nations. In most of those countries, by the year 2050, the median age of the population will approach fifty years.

The United States will gradually age but is distinctly younger than Japan and the European Union. One very surprising change is in Mexico. Traditionally a nation with a high birth rate, its rate has cascaded substantially in the past two decades, and people are living longer. The median age in Mexico is anticipated to double in the 2010–2050 time frame and will have the same median age in 2050 as the United States. And China and India are almost in the same age-gain mode.

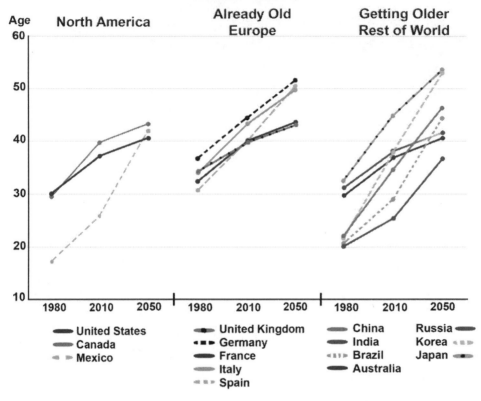

Figure 1.6

Median Age Projections
1980 - 2050

The culprit behind the median age gain is the fertility rate. For an industrialized nation to maintain a satisfactory economic-growth machine, it is necessary to have 2.0 births per female aged fifteen to forty-nine. This has been a keystone statistic for decades and has proven correct.

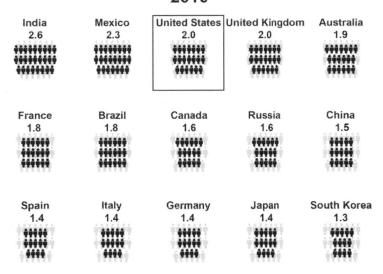

Figure 1.7

Fertility Rates
Major Industrialized Nations
2010

Fortunately, the United States maintains exactly a 2.0 rate, thanks largely to its Hispanic population and immigration. The European Union, China, Korea, Russia, and Japan have all fallen dramatically below that level. That low birth rate is contributing in large part to the inability of the European nations to recover from their most devastating recession in well over half a century.

Unlike China and Japan, the nations in the European Union each rely on their neighbors for purchases of the goods they produce. However, if all the nations in the Union have faltering populations, the situation will eventually be devastating. (Fortunately for Germany, its automobile manufacturing and exports save its day.)

Coinciding with the median age of the industrialized nations is the segment of the population that is under age fifteen. Of the total population of the United States, 20 percent is of that age. That is a relatively normal percentage for a nation with a 2.0 fertility rate.

Most European nations are well below the 20 percent level, the result of persons marrying later and having fewer children. The flight to fewer children is often attributed to the desire of middle-class households to better their economic condition. That is particularly true in economies where the unemployment rate is unduly high, as in Russia and the European nations.

Mexico—the United States' largest trading partner—has also had a substantial slowdown in births, thus its percentage of the population under age fifteen has fallen to an unprecedented low at 29 percent.

Nations whose under-age-fifteen population has fallen below 15 or 16 percent are in deep trouble.

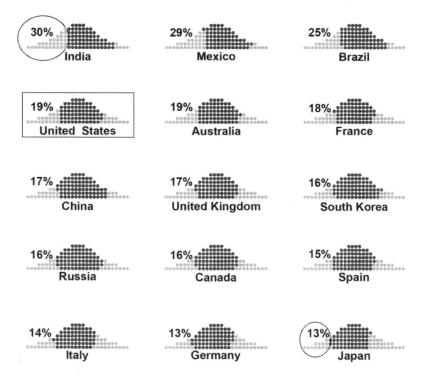

Figure 1.8a **Age Composition**
Major Industrialized Nations - Under 15
2010

30% India	29% Mexico	25% Brazil
19% United States	19% Australia	18% France
17% China	17% United Kingdom	16% South Korea
16% Russia	16% Canada	15% Spain
14% Italy	13% Germany	13% Japan

On the upper age ranges, Japan leads (in a bad way), with 23 percent of its population over age sixty-five. Germany and Italy follow closely behind, as does the rest of the European Union. In comparison, the United States is still relatively a nation of youths, with only 13 percent of its population over age sixty-five.

China, Mexico, Brazil, and India have the lowest percentages of folks over sixty-five of the fifteen nations I've analyzed.

Figure 1.8b Age Composition
Major Industrialized Nations - Over 65
2010

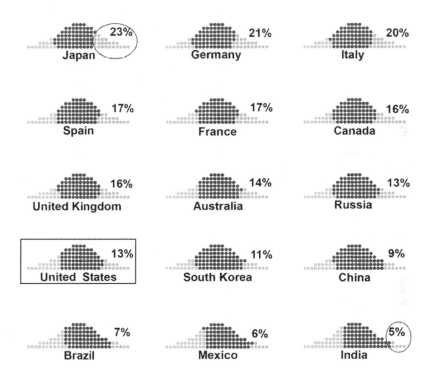

Think of the financial implications for nations like Japan that have an over-sixty-five population four times that of Mexico or India. Japan has had a faltering economy for almost a quarter century, and a good part of that unfortunate situation has to do with the nation's demography.

Think, too, in terms of the governmental obligations for paying into social-security and pension funds (both of which are substantially underfunded in the United States). And let us not forget the federal obligations for the health and care of the aging. Not a pretty picture.

If a nation wants a good future, it is imperative for it to have a strong birth rate, as it is the youth of today who will pay the bills for tomorrow (it is sort of like a Ponzi scheme). Thus, Japan and nations like Germany and Italy have very tough times ahead of them, as they are not reproducing in numbers that will allow them to prosper in the years ahead.

For countries like Japan, Germany, and Italy, long-term survival will depend on both increasing the birth rate and encouraging immigration from nations that have work ethics and education ethics for both men and women. A few countries qualify, like Russia, Bulgaria, Hungary, and Romania.

Nations that have stronger population gains tend to have greater economic expansion. Although the correlation is not perfect, there is a very noticeable relationship between the median age and the percentage change in the gross national income.

Figure 1.9

GNI % Growth & Median Age
2009-2014   2010

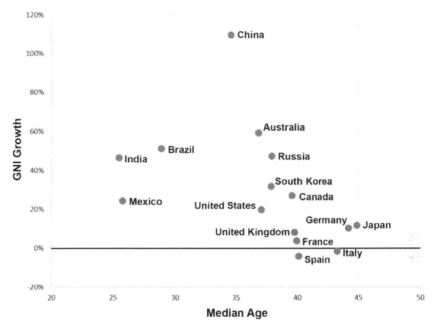

Germany, Japan, the United Kingdom, and Italy have the lowest birth rates and lowest amount of change in their gross national incomes. Conversely, nations with high birth rates tend to have the strongest economic-growth rates. Obviously, there are many other factors that go into the makeup of these nations' economics, but overall, there is rather strong evidence that in industrialized nations, more births means stronger economic expansion.

China has recently realized the folly of a one-child policy and is putting into effect programs to encourage more children. Korea is also aging far too rapidly and is just recognizing that stronger programs are needed to encourage its citizens to have more children.

Unfortunately, the effort to achieve an American-type middle-class lifestyle is the driving force for the paucity of childbirths in the nations that have a vision of household affluence.

As a capstone to this chapter, I have prepared a national rating chart that considers the multiple factors that go into a nation's success or eventual failure. Look at the chart through the eyes of an investor and think about which nation you would plow money into if you were seeking long-term gains, especially in real estate.

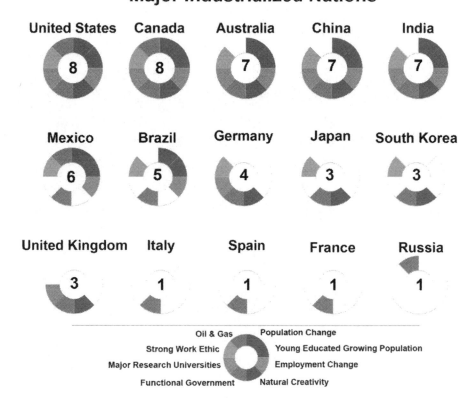

Figure 1.10

Strengths & Weaknesses
Major Industrialized Nations

United States — 8 Canada — 8 Australia — 7 China — 7 India — 7

Mexico — 6 Brazil — 5 Germany — 4 Japan — 3 South Korea — 3

United Kingdom — 3 Italy — 1 Spain — 1 France — 1 Russia — 1

Oil & Gas — Population Change
Strong Work Ethic — Young Educated Growing Population
Major Research Universities — Employment Change
Functional Government — Natural Creativity

Here's a snapshot of each of the fifteen industrialized nations. I should note that I have toured eleven of the fifteen nations over the past quarter century, discussed them with knowledgeable current or former residents, and have completed extensive research on all of them. The views are my own.

North America

United States

Still the envy of the world. It is growing, has good jobs, excellent college education, a strong work ethic, an enormous appetite for creativity, abundant oil and gas, a relatively functional federal government, and a brilliant future.

Canada

It is in as good a shape as the United States, has strong immigration from work-ethic nations on both coasts, and has a highly functional government. In addition, the country has excellent health care and is bulging with oil and gas. Canada doesn't make many headlines, and I guess its people like it that way. It has the same population as California, but, unlike California, has a government and leadership that exude common sense (regardless of which party is in power).

Mexico

A nation with incredible potential that just can't seem to shake off its third-world background. The nation is owned and operated by a handful of families, and the growth of the middle class and creativity are being stifled. But it will move forward, largely because of its proximity to the United States and a major supply of oil, competitive pricing of manufactured goods, and modern telecommunications. The drug cartels will remain, because the government doesn't have the will to fight them— but you have to take the good with the bad. You can't always choose your neighbors. Narcos forever. And corruption at the upper levels of government has never been higher. *Mordida* lives on.

European Nations

The lamps are going out all over Europe. We shall not see them lit again in our time.

—Sir Edward Gray, British foreign secretary
3 August 1914 (the eve of the World War I)

© Justin Cox

Germany

An absolute economic powerhouse. A nation that has re-created itself with a strong, commonsense government; enormous manufacturing capability; strong attraction for immigrants from nations to the east; and a very strong financial balance sheet. It is so strong that it really doesn't relate to the rest of the European Union.

The destruction of most of the nation's manufacturing capacity in World War II resulted in the generation of newer, modern technology and equipment. World War II not only destroyed the industrial sector, it also weakened the rigid social fabrics of the commercial and industrial bases and allowed the new nation to operate in a capitalistic mode. The new model propelled the development of a modern nation along US-style lines.

Germany will soon increase its population by almost a million persons from the Mid-East, few of whom, however, have the education levels and technical training needed to run the German tech machine. The situation should prove interesting. Absorbing East Germany was a piece of cake compared to this new venture. I suspect that Mr. and Mrs. Deutschland are not thrilled with this invasion.

United Kingdom

The United Kingdom needs to revive itself. It has just never recovered from World War II. Its manufacturing and production capacity are dismal. The country is, however, the heart of the financial world for Europe and is a safe haven for those escaping despotic nations. As English is the business language of the world England has the edge on the other European countries in terms of commandeering the world's financial institutions. It keeps on plugging along, but it needs a fresh burst of economic energy and a fertile native-British population.

Even though UK shocked the rest of the world with Brexit this year (2016), frankly it will mean little in the long run, but it will cut down the in-migration that natives consider unwanted. And, I suspect that was the primary reason for the 52/48 vote. Marvelous place for a vacation. I do hope Scotland doesn't secede.

Italy

What a wonderful country for tourism and manufacturing Ferraris and designer fashions. Unfortunately, its declining population and job base will lead to long-term woes, including high unemployment, a weak national economy, and a perpetually unstable government, simultaneously. And yet it appears that contacts and connections remain more important than talent in the job-seeking market. Unfortunately, the nation is sinking like Venice. Admittedly, most nations would kill for the Venetian and Roman tourist industries, and "made in Italy" still has a great cachet.

Spain

Another wonderful nation that has gone astray. The recent recession has been devastating to the economy and its job base. Tourism can only support so much of an economy. Slowly, Spain is becoming a manufacturing alternative to China and for the other European nations. It has so much to offer but desperately needs a massive dose of capitalism. Spain probably has the best opportunity to become an economic powerhouse and a star of the European economy. Unfortunately, it is still very difficult for young Spanish adults to get a job, almost as bad as France.

France

The most beautiful country in the world, with a capital that is, hands down, the most beautiful city in the world. Yet, France is dying. Its bent toward socialism, unfortunate presidential selections, and overwhelmingly out-of-control unions, along with massive immigration of uneducated and unproductive folks from poverty-stricken countries, will basically be the death of France. Especially if the far right preserver in near-term elections. Such a pity. It does have decent wine that is catching up in quality with that of the Napa Valley.

A distressing note on Europe: The Europe of today won't be the Europe of tomorrow. Borrowing a phrase from author Samuel P. Worthington, Europe has an "illusion of permanence." It is indeed an illusion and not a pretty one. Europe has a birthrate of 1.4 persons per household. The Islamic population in Europe averages four children per household and have their children much earlier in life. Thus, the Europe of tomorrow (particularly, Sweden, England and France) will have an entirely different demographic composition within a very few decades. And that does not augur well for the European Union.

The Other Super Nations

Australia

The best of the United Kingdom and the United States. It is a highly spirited nation, with strong population and employment growth, a vigorous work ethic, superb attitude, a lot of fuel, and good government. It is well placed in relation to China, Korea, and Japan.

China

Its growth has slowed, but it is a billion-plus-populated economic powerhouse with a government that is driven to succeed and has the monopolistic hegemonic power to mandate the necessary infrastructure and expenditures on education. No economic impact studies, community-planning groups, or Coastal Commission (a reference to California) there. China isn't heaven on earth, but both its government and its populace are highly capitalistic.

China will be the primary US partner for decades to come. Its economy is fragile because its households save up to 50 percent of their incomes, and therefore, consumer spending is far below what it should be. China's gross national savings rate is equal to more than 50 percent of its GDP. That compares to a US ratio of 12 percent. The US savings rate is closer to that of Uganda.

Note that if Walmart stopped buying goods from China for one month, China would be bankrupt. On the other hand, so would Walmart. This balance will keep the United States and China in bed together for a long time.

I should note that China is also at the forefront of corruption in government, harboring a situation in which government officials benefit mightily by grabbing pieces of growing companies. It's sort of fascinating. Government greatly encourages the growth of a multitude of companies because it is getting a piece of their action.

China has only one economic competitor of note in the future: India.

India

Another billion-plus meganation that is way behind China in almost everything but fertility but will work diligently to catch up. It needs to pull itself together with one language and one non-corrupt government, with a massive effort in education and infrastructure. This will not be easy, but China did it. India does have a very bright group of youngsters going through its education system, and the university system there is strong. Quite often, the brightest of the students come to US universities before returning to their home country.

There are really two Indias: India of the north, which is clearly a third-world country with a very high fertility rate and an inefficient, agricultural-based economy, and the India of the south, which is where the action is. Metropolitan areas like Delhi, Mumbai, Bangalore, and Kolkata are moving forward with zeal.

The caste system endures, but is gradually waning as the education level rises.

Brazil

Another third-world country that has the ability to move into second-world status. The people are bright, educable, and have a strong work ethic. And they are virtually energy independent. It is another nation that just needs to get its act together. There does appear to be a good deal of corruption at the higher levels of government, but that is not unusual for a South American country.

Japan

Another manufacturing mega-nation that is suffering badly because of a declining population and perpetual xenophobia. If it could entice its population to have more kids, it would be one of the three or four major forces in the future of the world. The Japanese do almost everything right except procreate. It is rumored that there are more diapers sold for seniors in Japan than for babies. Their overwhelming national debt doesn't help matters, either.

Korea

A totally remarkable nation that is a manufacturing machine but will suffer in the long term because of a low birth rate and relatively few people available to enter the workforce. It is a modern nation of unusually hard workers and a remarkable business ethic. It needs to acquire North Korea in a leveraged buyout. Goldman Sachs, BlackRock, and AIG are standing by.

One notable point: there is strong coordination between the government and industry (particularly the chaebols—business conglomerates) and, reportedly, government salaries are on par with those in industry. That means that the government is not the employer of last resort as it is in the United States.

Russia

It is fitting that Russia is at the bottom of the list. It is a nation that has nothing going for it but oil. Large segments of its educated population have moved out; the birth rate is plummeting, the median age is rising, and the government only cares about enriching itself. Things have been going wrong in Russia since Catherine the Great. And she died in 1797.

I should point out that the deaths of many of these nations are still a long way off. They die slowly, but they do die steadily. I have been exploring the demography and economies of these nations for many decades and find that the relevant trends are very difficult things to interrupt.

A final note: at some point, Indonesia and Singapore will become economic powerhouses. With some three hundred million persons (the world's fourth largest country), these nations, comprising thirteen thousand islands, will become a force rivaling China in terms of goods production. The area has oil and a population averaging under thirty years of age. It is working diligently to improve the literacy rate and has a capitalistic bent. And most business is conducted in English.

Having explored the major nations of the industrialized world in this chapter, we can now turn to the United States, a country that has both strong long-term population and employment prospects. And it is a pretty good place to live.

Chapter 2: The United States
An Exciting, Innovation Driven Nation

If you have freedom and energy, you can build a superpower nation.

—Barack Obama

In the next chapters, I will discuss a broad range of topics regarding the fifty United States and many of the country's metropolitan areas, segmenting them into those that will prosper and those that won't: this is the "great divide."

We are blessed in the United States because our population is growing. Population growth drives the economy because two-thirds of the gross domestic product (GDP) consists of people and businesses buying things. The United States is a consumer economy and has been since the end of World War II. New population creates new jobs and the need for new housing.

Between 2010 and 2040, the US population is projected to grow by seventy-one million—almost 2.5 million people annually. Notably, however, population growth is slowing somewhat. In the 1950–1980 period, the United States expanded its population by 50 percent, and then in the 1980–2010 period, 36 percent. It is anticipated to grow 23 percent in the 2010–2040 period. While the percentages now is lower than the past, the United States continues to grow by more than two million people annually.

Figure 2.1

Population Change United States 1980-2040			
Year	**1980**	**2010**	**2040 (P)**
Population	226,545,805	308,745,538	380,016,000
Change from 30 Years	75,848,444	82,199,733	71,270,462
Decennial Change	25,282,815	27,399,911	23,756,821
Annual Change	2,528,281	2,739,991	2,375,682
% from Past 30 Yrs.	**50%**	**36%**	**23%**

The US non-Hispanic white population is projected to shrink slightly in the 2010–2040 period because its members are marrying later and having fewer children. US growth will be fueled by the populations of Hispanics, Asians, and blacks (this is how the Census Bureau refers to those whom we now call African Americans. The census does have a separate category for blacks who were born in Africa and doesn't want the two confused). Please note that in the census, respondents self-describe their ethnicities. That is why in the table below, the "other" category has six million-plus people in it and is growing rapidly. A second reason for that "other" category growing substantially is that many people report themselves as bi-ethnic. After all, our nation is the epitome of population assimilation.

We are most fortunate to be in a nation that has proven highly attractive to Hispanics and Asians, as their immigration here over the past few decades has been our economic saving grace. In the 2010–2040 time frame, the nation is projected to add almost fifty million Hispanics and more than ten million Asians, most of whose families have, in fact, have already been here for decades.

If it were not for the Hispanics and Asians, we would be in the same sinking boat as Russia, Japan, and most of the European nations.

Figure 2.2

Total Population Change by Ethnicity United States 1980-2040		
Ethnicity	**1980-2010**	**2010-2040**
Non-Hispanic White	16,561,186	(2,930,552)
Hispanic	35,868,921	44,398,406
Asian	11,173,813	11,206,748
Black	12,434,294	9,839,681
Other	6,161,519	8,756,179
Total	**82,199,733**	**71,270,462**

When we look at the total composition of our nation, we can see the non-Hispanic white population declining from 80 percent in 1980 to barely half by 2040. The Hispanic population will substitute for the lost non-Hispanic white population numbers. Thus, the Hispanic population by 2040 will have expanded from 6.4 percent of the population to 25 percent.

Figure 2.3

Changing Ethnicity of Population United States 1980-2040 (F)			
Ethnicity	1980	2010	2040
Non-Hispanic White	79.6%	63.7%	51.0%
Hispanic	6.4%	16.3%	25.0%
Asian	1.5%	4.8%	6.8%
Black	11.7%	12.6%	12.8%
Other	0.8%	2.6%	4.4%
Total	100.0%	100.0%	100.0%

Thus, in the 2010–2040 time frame, almost two-thirds of the population gain in the nation will be Hispanic, with 15 percent Asian, 14 percent black, and 12 percent other and a combination of other ethnic groups.

Figure 2.4

Ethnicity: Percent of Total Population Change United States 1980-2040		
Ethnicity	1980-2010	2010-2040
Non-Hispanic White	20.1%	-4.1%
Hispanic	43.6%	62.3%
Asian	13.6%	15.7%
Black	15.1%	13.8%
Other	7.5%	12.3%
Total	100.0%	100.0%

The blessing of the two major immigrant groups (Hispanic and Asian) is that they have very strong work ethics, are hungry for success, and have only migrated here to become part of the nation's economic machine. Further, after one generation, they are typically assimilated into American society and enjoy the fruits of their labor.

I will discuss the geographic distribution of the future population in a later chapter.

Aging Patterns

The nation is growing older, but the rate is nowhere near the pace of the European nations or Japan. Nonetheless, the median age here is now 37.2 years. Notably, the pattern of aging started a century ago. In 1900, the median age was twenty-three years.

Similarly, because of falling birth rates, the percent of the nation that is under age fifteen has shrunk from 35 percent in 1900 to 21 percent at the time of the 2010 census. Like the median age, the pattern has been progressive.

Similarly, the over-sixty-five population has gradually risen from 4 percent in 1900 to 13 percent in 2010. The sixty-five-and-older crowd has been growing because folks are living longer and are healthier and, for the most part, have jobs that do not cause inhalation of noxious fumes, including cigarette smoke. Further, the United States has made major strides in the field of medicine and pharmaceuticals that also result in longer and better-quality life—"better living through chemistry."

Figure 2.5

Aging Patterns United States 1950-2010				
	Percent of Population			
Age Range	**1900**	**1950**	**1980**	**2010**
Under 15	35%	27%	23%	21%
65 and Older	4%	8%	11%	13%
Median Age	**22.90**	**30.20**	**30.00**	**37.2**

Source: U.S. Census

The slowing of US growth is also a function of age at marriage. An interesting trend was that age at marriage had been on a downward bent through 1950. Thus, the female population at the age of marriage was 22.0 in 1900; it dropped to 20.3 in 1950 and then rose dramatically to the 26.1 it is now.

Thus, from 1950 through 2010, the male age at marriage has gained 24 percent and that of brides, 28 percent.

Figure 2.6

Age at Marriage United States 1900-2010		
Year	Men	Women
1900	25.9	22.0
1930	24.3	21.3
1950	22.8	20.3
1980	24.7	22.0
2010	28.2	26.1

Women and Minorities in the Workforce

There are two primary reasons for this phenomenon. The first is the major increase of women in the workforce and, concomitantly, the percentage of women attending college.

In 1950, women were only 20 percent of total employment. Those were the *Leave It to Beaver* days, when many considered a woman's place was exclusively in the home and her primary role in life was to have children, cook and care for her spouse and loving family. Obviously, that situation has changed—a lot. Now, women compose almost half of total employment. Thus, since 1950, women have gained more than fifty million jobs.

Figure 2.7

Civilian Labor Force and Employment United States 1950-2010		
Year	Females Employed	Female as % of Total Employed
1950	12,000	20.0%
1980	41,300	42.4%
2010	65,500	47.1%
(1) persons over 16 years of age		
source: U.S. Statistical Abstract		

While the 1950's culture had women's role in society being at home, a decade earlier during World War II had women brought into the workforce in droves and substituted for men in traditionally male work. After the war though, the men returned and most women left to become mothers (of baby boomers) or were pushed out.

The years following 1950, a major part of the increase in jobs for women has been the dramatic change in the types of jobs available. In the postwar years, the advent of female-friendly jobs exploded with the expansion of industries and positions that required more brains than brawn. In the same time period there was a cultural shift in the role of women.

As new industries and jobs materialized in the 1970's and 1980's, female college education accelerated. As a result, the entire US employment agenda changed.

The age of marriage and the female labor-participation rate go hand in hand. (I should note that the 1990 census was the first one that did not have a category for women's work called "keeping house.")

Figure 2.8

Age of Marriage and Labor Participation Rate United States 1950-2010		
Year	Age of Marriage - Women	Labor Participation Rate
1950	20.3	33.0%
1960	20.3	37.7%
1970	20.6	43.3%
1980	22.0	51.2%
1990	23.9	57.4%
2000	25.1	59.5%
2010	26.0	58.2%

source: U.S. Census Bureau

In terms of education, women composed 20.3 percent of high-school graduates entering college in 1970. By 2010, the percentage had more than doubled. And, related to that, the total percentage of high-school graduates entering college increased 60 percent from 1970 to 2010.

The 60 percent increase is vitally important, given the expanding breadth of jobs that have been created since the 1970's. Basically, the entirety of the software, biotech/life sciences, social media and telecommunications industries emerged only in the past third of a century.

(I should mention that women and men do not differ in IQ. There is no reason that women shouldn't be able to compete on an equal footing in these new industries. There can be no debate on that issue.)

Figure 2.9

Enrollment Rate of 18-24 Year Olds in Degree-Granting Institutions By Sex United States 1970-2010			
	% of HS Graduates Entering College		
		Sex	
Year	Total, all students	Male	Female
1970	25.7	32.1	20.3
1990	32.0	32.3	31.8
2010	41.2	38.3	44.1
% Change 1970-2010	60%	19%	117%

Source: Current Population Survey as of August 2011

Perhaps as notable is the massive increase in blacks and Hispanics attending degree-granting institutions. In 1970, only 15 percent of black high-school graduates entered college. By 2010, that percentage has more than doubled. The Hispanic percentage has almost tripled from 13 percent in 1970 to 38 percent in 2010.

Asian students have always cherished higher education; almost two-thirds of US Asian students enter college.

Figure 2.10

Enrollment Rate of 18-24 Year Olds in Degree-Granting Institutions United States 1970-2010				
	% of HS Graduates Entering College			
Year	White	Black	Hispanic	Asian
1970	27.5%	15.4%	13.4%	(1)
1990	35.1%	25.4%	15.8%	56.9%
2010	43.1%	38.4%	38.4%	63.6%
% Change 1970-2010	56.7%	149.6%	186.9%	

(1) in 1970, Asians were not tabulated
Source: Current Population Survey as of August 2011

Household Spending Patterns

From an economic standpoint, the collegiate education of women and their rising employment and self-sufficiency have been the primary reasons that our consumer society has prospered. Single, educated women without children tend to have major spending power. They are also the driving force in the purchases of automobiles, furniture, clothing, travel, and recreational goods.

And then, the rise of the two-job household with fewer children caused a massive unleashing of consumer spending that has seen the creation of rapidly expanding choices in goods.

I remember a scene in the movie *Moscow on the Hudson*, where a recent immigrant from Russia (played by Robin Williams) passes out in the aisle of a supermarket, swooning at the incredible selection of merchandise.

The first supermarkets were five-to-ten thousand square feet in size and now are in the fifty-thousand-to-ninety-thousand-square-foot range. A loaf of bread once meant bland Wonder Bread. Bagels, brioche, and baguettes were unknown outside of New York and Los Angeles.

A regional shopping center of one million-plus square feet would not have been possible fifty years ago because the myriad of stores that we now take for granted did not yet exist. Further, as many as 90 percent of the stores in regional shopping centers have goods aimed directly at the female shopper.

In the same vein, the entire realm of upscale merchandise for the masses has been created since women returned to the workforce. The next time you walk through a regional shopping center, count the number of stores that are upscale and directed toward the female shopper, starting, of course, with Nordstrom and Bloomingdale's. And, simultaneously, mull over the chains that are aimed at the middle class and are suffering or have disappeared from the retail landscape: Sears, Montgomery Ward, Mervyns, and Kmart, among others.

In the Washington, DC, area, great department-store names like Hecht's, Lansburgh's, Woodward & Lothrop, and Garfinckel's are now just part of history.

Household Size

Tied in with the upward bent of American shopping habits is the decline in persons per household. It's very difficult to load up your cart at Nordstrom when you are dragging along three or four kids. At the beginning of the twentieth century, the number of people per household was 4.6. By 2010, it had declined to 2.6.

Figure 2.11

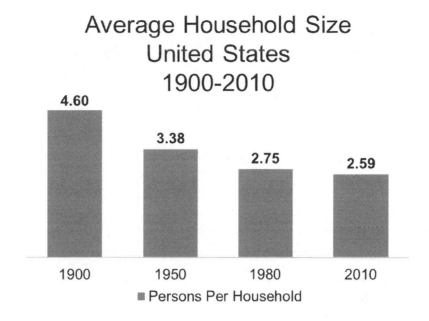

The three most radical changes have been in the number of households with five or more persons and of one- and two-person households. The percent of households with five or more children has had a stunning decline of 80 percent since 1900, with most of it occurring in the 1900–1950 period. The steady increase in one- and two-person households has also been exceptional. These have increased from 20 percent of total households to more than 60 percent.

The primary reasons for the gain in one- and two-person households relate back to the increase in people going to college, marrying later, having children later, and, for singles, being able to afford to live alone. In cities like New York, London, and Paris, the percent of those living by themselves is pushing the 50 percent level. Millennials just "want to be alone"—at least for a little while.

Figure 2.12

Households by Size United States 1900-2010				
	% of Households			
No. Persons	**1900**	**1950**	**1980**	**2010**
1-Person	5.1%	9.3%	22.7%	27.0%
2-Person	15.2%	28.1%	31.3%	33.9%
3-Person	17.8%	22.8%	17.4%	16.0%
4-Person	17.2%	18.4%	15.4%	13.8%
5 or Persons	44.7%	21.4%	13.2%	9.4%
Total	100.0%	100.0%	100.0%	100.0%
1 & 2 Person HHs	**20.3%**	**37.4%**	**54.0%**	**60.9%**

Let me focus further on the one- and two-person households just because of the enormousness of the number. In the 1980–2010 period, one- and two-person households increased by twenty-eight million. One-person households alone increased by thirteen million.

Think of these numbers in terms of the types of housing necessary to fulfill the needs of those one- and two-person households. As most of the increase is urban, also think of it in terms of needs in transportation, recreation, entertainment, and personal services.

Think about how many pet-care, dog-walking, yoga, tanning, and hair and nail-polish salons you pass every day in an urban setting. Entire new industries have been created to satisfy those small households living in an urban setting and with a solid income. And, while you are at it, think about how many of those services are provided by Hispanics and Asians. Where would we be without them and their probusiness inventiveness?

Figure 2.13

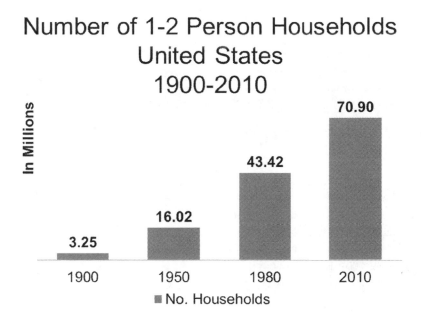

Number of 1-2 Person Households
United States
1900-2010

In Millions

3.25	16.02	43.42	70.90
1900	1950	1980	2010

■ No. Households

As a correlative of the increase in the age of marriage and in the number who go to college, we can look at the fertility rate of the nation. The fertility rate is a function of national happiness, which is also a function of the state of the economy and the one-time game changer: the birth-control pill.

The Census Bureau typically defines fertility rate as births per one thousand women aged fifteen to forty-four. During World War II, the average fertility rate was 82.4. Then the rate jumped to 114.0 as Americans "put on a happy face." Then came 1964, when we were in mourning for the death of a president, the expansion of Vietnam warfare, and, most important, the FDA's approval of the birth-control pill. Those three factors drove down the fertility rate to 86.4 in the 1964–1973 period.

From 1974 to 1987, the birth rate stabilized at 66.4 and then started to rise with the booming, Reagan-propelled economy. Thus, in 1988–1992, the fertility rate rose to 69.2 but then declined as a result of a recession, higher gas prices, a depressed housing market, and substantial job losses in the service sector. The boom of 2003–2007 started a fertility expansion, which was doing quite well until 2008, when the economy crashed big-time. Since 2008, the birth rate has declined to a post–World War II low of 63.8.

Figure 2.14

Fertility Rate and the Economy Births per 1,000 Women Aged 15-44 United States 1940-2013	
World War II	82.4
1946-1963 (Post-War Boom)	114.0
1964-1973 (Pill Approved; JFK Killed; Viet Nam)	86.4
1974-1987 (Nixon Resigns; Reagan Elected, Viet Nam ends)	66.4
1988-1992 (Reagan, Booming Economy)	69.2
1993-2002 (Birth Rates Stabilize)	65.7
2003-2007 (Economic boom)	67.4
2008-2013 (The Big Recession)	63.8

Urbanization

And, on the topic of urban settings, the percent of Americans living in them has increased dramatically in recent decades and will continue to do so. In the 1900–1950 period, as we rapidly moved from an agricultural nation to a manufacturing one, the number of people moving to the cities doubled in terms of people per square mile. Since then, it has almost doubled again, with persons per square mile reaching the 87 percent level by 2010.

Figure 2.15

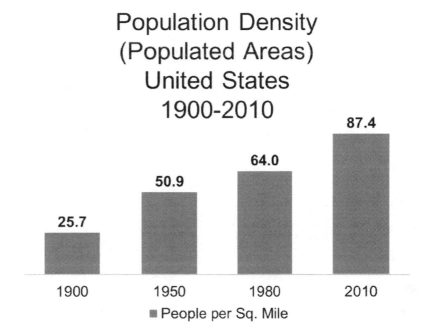

Population Density
(Populated Areas)
United States
1900-2010

87.4

64.0

50.9

25.7

| 1900 | 1950 | 1980 | 2010 |

■ People per Sq. Mile

A Political Statement

The twentieth century clearly belonged to the United States. It had great industrial and economic strength and, very often, superb leadership that understood how to wield power and bring friendly nations together and save the world from catastrophes. The twenty-first century may be different. Contributing to the changes are the globalization of manufacturing, transportation, and information. In this century, economic and financial power are somewhat more equitably distributed around the world.

Scholar Daniel Gouré writes in In Focus Magazine that "national power is not the same as leadership." The United States still has the power (military, fiscal, and economic), but its international leadership in recent years has been lacking.

The next quarter century will determine if the United States can once again assume the leadership that is mandatory to hold the world together.

We must be the powerful orchestra leader. We certainly can't leave the leadership to Russia or China.

> **Conclusion: America continues to grow, but in unequal ways. The Hispanic and Asian population will grow faster than others. Population density continues to increase however household size continues to shrink and people are marrying later in life. It is still a young country.**

Chapter 3: The State of the States
The Great Divide

The best way to predict the future is to create it.

—Peter Drucker

It's nice to think that all US states are created equal. But, like citizens, in practice, they are not. If there is a key theme to this book, it is that not only are states not all created equal, but the inequalities between them are expanding.

In this book, I concentrate on the thirty-six states that contain 95 percent of the US population. The other fourteen states, plus the District of Columbia, contain only 5.2 percent of the nation's three hundred million-plus people (so, less than two million). Some may grow greatly in population someday, but not in the near future.

Admittedly, I like most of these mini-states, but their effect on the future of the United States will be minimal. Yes, I know that Wyoming, West Virginia, and North Dakota have a lot of coal and oil and some pretty scenery, but this book is about population and the future expansion of this nation. Demographics are our destiny. (Plus, from a statistical standpoint, it is easier to deal with thirty-six states than fifty.)

The following page is a snapshot of the fourteen mini-states and DC:

Figure 3.1

States with Fewer than 2,000,000 Population United States 2010		
State	No.	Population
Alaska	1	710,231
Delaware	2	897,934
District of Columbia	3	601,723
Hawaii	4	1360301
Idaho	5	1,567,582
Maine	6	1,328,361
Montana	7	989,415
Nebraska	8	1,826,341
New Hampshire	9	1,316,470
North Dakota	10	672,591
Rhode Island	11	1,052,567
South Dakota	12	814,180
Vermont	13	625,741
West Virginia	14	1,852,994
Wyoming	15	563,626
Total		16,180,057
U.S. Population		308,745,538
% of U.S. Population		5.2%

In this book, I segment the nation into six regions: Northeast, Midwest, Southeast, West, Mountain, and Texas. I know that Texas is not exactly a region, but it is a world unto itself, much like California, but in a different sort of way. (As I've mentioned, California is really more of a state of mind than a state—but more on that later.)

Since 1950, the United States has more than doubled in size, now topping out at more than 300 million.

In the 1950–1980 period, we added seventy-four million people, and then from 1980 to 2010, we added another eighty-one million. Big numbers. Big country.

As I alluded to earlier, not all the states are the same, and certainly not all the regions are, either. The West, Southeast, Mountain states, and Texas have far outpaced the growth of the Midwest and Northeast. The four growth regions accounted for 60 percent of the nation's population gains in the 1950–1980 period and then jumped to 75 percent of total gains in the 1980–2010 time frame. Thus, of the eighty-one million added to the nation's population in the 1980–2010 period, sixty-one million were in the West, Southeast, Mountain, and Texas.

Figure 3.2

Population Change by Region Continental United States 1950-2010									
	Thousands								
	Population			Change 1950-2010		Change 1950-1980		Change 1980-2010	
Region	1950	1980	2010	Change	% Change	Change	% Change	Change	% Change
West	16,077	35,254	58,961	42,884	266.7%	19,177	119.3%	23,707	67.2%
Texas	7,711	14,229	25,145	17,434	226.1%	6,518	84.5%	10,916	76.7%
Mountain	3,484	6,551	10,913	7,429	213.2%	3,067	88.0%	4,362	66.6%
Southeast	26,445	42,768	65,385	38,940	147.2%	16,323	61.7%	22,617	52.9%
Midwest	54,840	72,429	84,279	29,439	53.7%	17,589	32.1%	11,850	16.4%
Northeast	42,139	53,946	61,988	19,849	47.1%	11,807	28.0%	8,042	14.9%
Total	150,696	225,177	306,671	155,975	103.5%	74,481	49.4%	81,494	36.2%
West, Texas, Mtn., SE as % of Total	35.6%	43.9%	52.3%	68.4%		60.5%		75.6%	

In fact, just fourteen states in the nation accounted for almost three-quarters of the nation's population gain in the 1980–2010 period. And three states alone—California, Texas, and Florida accounted for 57 percent of the nation's growth in the past thirty years.

Figure 3.3

States with More than 1.5% Annual Population Gain States with More than 2,000,000 Population United States 1980-2010					
				1980-2010	
States	1980	2010	1980-2010	% change	Annual %
United States	226,545,805	308,745,538	82,199,733	36.3%	1.2%
California	23,667,902	37,253,956	13,586,054	57%	1.9%
Texas	14,229,191	25,145,561	10,916,370	77%	2.6%
Florida	9,746,324	18,801,310	9,054,986	93%	3.1%
Georgia	5,463,105	9,687,653	4,224,548	77%	2.6%
Arizona	2,718,215	6,392,017	3,673,802	135%	4.5%
North Carolina	5,881,766	9,535,483	3,653,717	62%	2.1%
Virginia	5,346,818	8,001,024	2,654,206	50%	1.7%
Washington	4,132,156	6,724,540	2,592,384	63%	2.1%
Colorado	2,889,964	5,029,196	2,139,232	74%	2.5%
Nevada	800,493	2,700,551	1,900,058	237%	7.9%
South Carolina	3,121,820	4,625,364	1,503,544	48%	1.6%
Utah	1,461,037	2,763,885	1,302,848	89%	3.0%
Oregon	2,633,105	3,831,074	1,197,969	45%	1.5%
New Mexico	1,302,894	2,059,179	756,285	58%	1.9%
Total	83,394,790	142,550,793	59,156,003	71%	2.4%
% of U.S. Population Growth	36.8%	46.2%	72.0%		

The map that follows points out rather vividly where the nation's growth is heading:

Figure 3.4 – **The Great Divide**

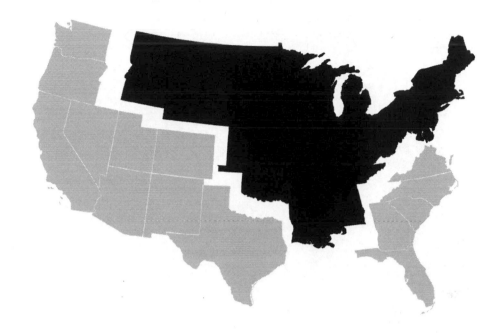

Every decade, the Census Bureau calculates the population center of the
United States. Notably, every year since 1790, the population center has
moved south and west. In 1790, the population center was in the great
state of Maryland but is now in the southern part of Missouri. The
progress from east to south and west is steady, dependable, and inevitable.
Note that since 1950, there has been a definite bent toward the south.

Figure 3.5

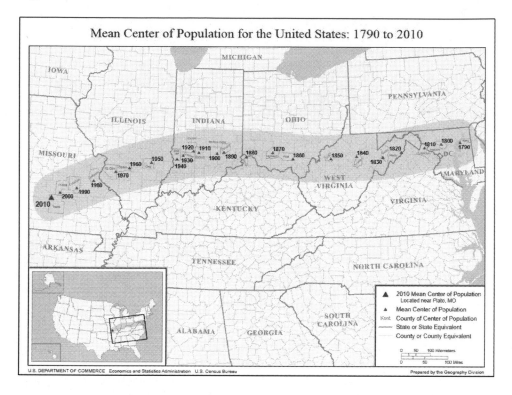

The expectation is that the trend will continue. The Weldon Cooper Institute at the University of Virginia has projected state population out to 2040, and the future looks strangely like the past. The Institute projects that 78 percent of the nation's population gains will be in Texas, the West, the Southeast, and the Mountain states. A paltry 22 percent of total gain will be in the Midwest and the Northeast.

Figure 3.6

	Thousands			
	Population			
Region	2010	2040	Change	% Change
West	58,961	80,808	21,847	37.1%
Texas	25,145	35,250	10,105	40.2%
Mountain	10,913	14,932	4,019	36.8%
Southeast	65,385	85,471	20,086	30.7%
Midwest	84,279	93,968	9,689	11.5%
Northeast	61,988	69,008	7,020	11.3%
Total	306,671	379,437	72,766	23.7%
West, Texas, Mtn., SE as % of Total	52.3%	57.0%	77.0%	

Population Change by Region Continental United States 2010-2040

There are nine key factors that caused these fourteen states to lead the way to accelerated future growth. They are:

- Good air
- Air conditioning
- Air travel
- Congressional representation
- Federal Funding
- Union membership
- Economic freedom
- Hispanic growth
- Absence of social rigidity

Good Air

Mary Walshok, Vice Chancellor of UC San Diego, states that the start of the sunbelt movement was in the early 1900's as persons suffering from lung diseases created by the smoke-belching industries of the Mid-west started moving south and west to improve their breathing.

Air Conditioning

It's sort of strange how one invention can change a nation. In 1917, Willis Carrier installed air conditioning in a movie theater. This innovation caused the movie industry to blossom as much as, if not more, than the addition of "talkies" did.

The air-conditioning industry was just getting underway big-time when the recession hit. Then there was World War II. Thus, the modern air-conditioning industry didn't gain momentum until the late 1940s. Harry Truman was the first president to have an air-conditioned car. And the White House wasn't fully air conditioned until the mid-1930s.

If it were not for Willis Carrier, all the states south of the Mason-Dixon line would never have prospered and certainly wouldn't have the thousands of high-rise condominiums and office towers that blanket them today.

Before air conditioning, there really wasn't a South or a Texas. Their states were minor forces, most often dependent on farming, tobacco, or livestock for their livelihoods—not much different than right after the Civil War. True, some homes there did have electricity and indoor plumbing, but certainly there were none of the accoutrements that a modern metropolitan area demands.

Air Travel

Many of us have probably seen old movies showing the PanAm Clipper crossing from New York to London right before World War II. The plane was elegant, held thirty-seven passengers, and flew at 188 miles per hour. Improvements in air travel were slow, though, until 1955, when Boeing introduced the 707, initiating the jet age. Ten years later, it launched the 747, and air travel expanded exponentially after that.

In 1951, Pan American Airways racked up 1,551 million passenger miles. Forty years later, that figure had increased twenty times.

It would be hard to imagine the population of California, Texas, and Florida expanding to their present enormous sizes without the ability to fly there. I have driven from the East Coast to California in a car without air conditioning. It ain't fun.

Congressional Representation

Each congressional district represents approximately seven hundred thousand people. The changing distribution of congressional seats has had a powerful effect on the nation's economies.

The effect of a disproportionate gain has a massive effect on where the federal government spends its money, because more population means more congressional representation. We have 435 congressional seats to divvy up, and the piñata explodes with federal dollars for regions with rising population.

Since 1950, the seating arrangement has changed radically. In 1950, the seating was two-thirds for the colder states and one-third for the warmer ones. In 2010, warmth beat out cold 53 percent to 47 percent. And the future holds more of the same. Thus, since 1950, the cold states have lost seventy-six seats, and the warm ones gained them. Easy math.

Figure 3.7

Congressional Representation by Region United States 1950-2010			
Region	1950	1980	2010
Midwest	158	139	118
Mountain	11	14	15
Northeast	123	104	87
Southeast	75	80	92
Texas	22	27	36
West	46	68	84
Alaska/Hawaii	0	3	3
Total	435	435	435
Mountain, Southeast, Texas and West	154	192	230
% of Total	35%	44%	53%
Northeast and Midwest	281	243	205
% of Total	65%	56%	47%

And, as you might suspect, a few states (California, Texas, Florida, and Georgia) cut a fat hog, doubling their representation in the past sixty years. Conversely, the states of Illinois, Michigan, New York, Ohio, and Pennsylvania collectively lost forty-six seats.

Figure 3.8

Congressional Representation Key States 1950-2010				
	1950	1980	2010	Change 1950-2010
State	No. Reps	No. Reps	No. Reps	
California	30	45	53	23
Florida	8	19	27	19
Georgia	10	10	14	4
Texas	22	27	36	14
Total Winners	70	101	130	60
Illinois	25	22	18	-7
Michigan	18	18	14	-4
New York	43	34	27	-16
Ohio	23	21	16	-7
Pennsylvania	30	23	18	-12
Total Losers	139	118	93	-46

Federal Largess

Highway Funds

He or she who holds the congressional purse strings allocates funds according to the number of seats held. As an example, look at highway-fund allocations. Approximately one-third of total allocations goes to five states: California, Texas, Florida, Pennsylvania, and New York.

Figure 3.9

Highway Fund Allocations Key States with 4% or More of Total 2013		
State	Allocation	% of Total
California	$ 3,546,492,430	9.5%
Texas	$ 3,049,292,304	8.1%
Florida	$ 1,830,766,277	4.9%
New York	$ 1,621,928,778	4.3%
Pennsylvania	$ 1,585,402,148	4.2%
Total	$ 11,633,881,937	31.0%
Total	$ 37,476,819,674	100.0%

NASA Funds

NASA funds are distributed in a similar manner. Almost two-thirds of total funding goes to the Southeast, Texas, and the West. Only 20 percent goes to the cold parts of the country. One reason is that launches closer to the equator are more efficient. Also admittedly, it is a little difficult to shoot missiles during ice storms, but the proportion is still a bit more uneven than one might expect.

Figure 3.10

Distribution of NASA Funds By Region 2013		
Southeast/Texas/West	$	8,279
Midwest/Northeast	$	2,810
Mountain	$	1,969
Alaska/Hawaii	$	39
Total	$	13,097
Southeast/Texas/West		63.2%
Midwest/Northeast		21.5%
Mountain		15.0%
Alaska/Hawaii		0.3%
Total		100.0%

Department of Defense

In the same vein, allocation of funds from the Department of Defense have a similar pattern, with the Southeast, Texas, Mountain states, and the West grabbing six of every ten dollars spent.

Figure 3.11

Distribution of Funds Payroll and Contracts Department of Defense 2009			
Region	**No. States**	**Per State**	**Totals**
Southeast/Texas/West	12	$ 24,764,672	$ 297,176,063
Midwest/Northeast	22	$ 9,052,589	$ 199,156,962
Mountain	2	$ 4,447,987	$ 8,895,974
Alaska/Hawaii	14	$ 977,787	$ 13,689,017
Total	50	$ 10,378,360	$ 518,918,016
Southeast/Texas/West	17		57.3%
Midwest/Northeast	27		38.4%
Mountain	5		1.7%
Alaska/Hawaii	2		2.6%
Total	51		100.0%

In short, federal spending indicates a lot about where the future growth of the United States is headed.

Union Membership

There is a direct and potent inverse correlation between regional growth and union membership.

Nationally, union membership as a percent of total employment has been in a declining state since the 1970s. In 1980, one-third of the employment base was unionized. Today, that figure has dipped to 10 percent.

There are six primary reasons for this phenomenon:

- Manufacturing employment has moved from union states to nonunion states
- Most employment gains have been made in small companies, which are traditionally too difficult for unions to organize

- Major employment gains have been in industries that are very difficult to unionize, among them biotech, telecommunications, high-tech manufacturing, and specialty production facilities
- Robotics have dramatically increased productivity (i.e., there is less need for employees)
- Unions do not have much appeal to college-educated employees
- Unions have proven to be more of an impediment than an assist to individual incentives

Figure 3.12

Union Membership as % of Total Employment United States 1980-2013			
Year	Employment (000)	Members (000)	% Memb
1980	20,850	6,726	32.3%
1990	20,339	4,197	20.6%
2000	19,167	2,832	14.8%
2013	14,188	1,429	10.1%

Source: Hirsch/MacPherson (from Current Population Survey)

Manufacturing jobs, the historic heart of our economy, have tended to move to the nonunion states, as shown in the table below. The fourteen fast-growing states have a union proportion of 6 percent of all manufacturing jobs, while the other states have 12 percent.

Figure 3.13

Percent Union Membership Manufacturing Industries Fast Growing and Other States States with More than 2,000,000 Population	
Category	% Union
Fast Growing States	6%
Other States	12%

On a regional basis, private-industry union membership in the fastest-growing states has slipped to the 2 to 3 percent level, while in the Midwest and Northeast, it is two to three times that percentage.

The West still has a high rate of union membership because of major aeronautical and military production in the states of Washington and California.

Figure 3.14

Private Industry Union Membership as % of Total Employment By Region States with more than 2,000,000 Population 2013			
Region	Total Employment	Union Membership	% Union
Northeast	24,599,702	2,050,351	8%
West	23,583,806	1,667,793	7%
Midwest	33,950,958	2,256,024	7%
Mountain	3,494,117	119,693	3%
Southeast	25,614,284	597,160	2%
Texas	10,880,079	242,686	2%
Total U.S	122,122,946	6,933,707	6%

Table 3.15 summarizes the relationship between population and employment growth and union membership. Other than the West Coast, the other eleven fast-growing states have half the percentage of union membership than the twenty-four slow-growing states.

Figure 3.15

Ratio of Population, Employment Growth and Union Membership United States, by State 1980 and 2013			
State	% Union 2013	Annual Pop. Change 1980-2010	Empl. Growth 1980-2013
West Coast	16%	1.8%	67%
Other Fast Growing States	6%	3.0%	99%
Balance of States	11%	0.6%	33%

In his seminal book *The Rise and Decline of Nations*, Mancur Olson says, "Unions are the main organizations with negative effects on local growth and their membership should also serve as a proxy measure of the strength of such other coalitions that are harmful to local growth." (He notes that the number of lawyers per one hundred thousand people is also a dependable indicator of growth inhibitors.)

Economic Freedom

Economic freedom is a topic that is rarely reported as a reason for economic growth, yet it is a powerful analytical tool. George Mason University in Virginia produces an economic-freedom rating of the fifty US states. The rating is based on three factors: economic freedom, regulatory policy, and fiscal policy. The West Coast of this nation does not fare very well on the overall freedom ranking, with Washington, Oregon, and California particularly weak in the economic-freedom category. Basically, their growth has been amazing *despite* the weakness of their economic freedom.

Six of the top fourteen growth states are in the top ten of economic-freedom ratings. Almost all of the fourteen fastest-growing states are in the top half of the higher-economic-freedom states.

In total overall rating, the fourteen growth states have an average score of 12 (the top quarter of all states).

Figure 3.16

State Rating of Freedom Fastest Growing States 36 States with a More than 2,000,000 Population				
State	**Overall Freedom Ranking**	**Economic Freedom**	**Regulatory Policy**	**Fiscal Policy**
California	34	35	34	34
Washington	32	32	33	30
Oregon	20	28	28	21
Colorado	1	1	8	3
Texas	2	3	19	2
Arizona	5	7	10	10
Virginia	6	9	12	9
Utah	7	10	6	14
Georgia	12	2	7	5
Florida	16	18	13	19
North Carolina	17	19	18	15
Nevada	18	17	24	8
South Carolina	22	16	9	27
New Mexico	26	33	27	35
Average	**12**	**12**	**14**	**13**

"Freedom in the 50 States" ; Mercatus Center, George Mason University, 2009

Interesting enough, there is a very strong correlation between high scores on overall freedom and low percentages of union membership, as shown below:

Figure 3.17

State Rating of Freedom Fastest Growing States 36 States with a More than 2,000,000 Population		
State	**Overall Freedom Ranking**	**% Union Membership**
West Coast		
California	34	16%
Washington	32	19%
Oregon	20	14%
Non-West Coast		
Colorado	1	8%
Texas	2	5%
Arizona	5	7%
Virginia	6	5%
Utah	7	4%
Georgia	12	5%
Florida	16	5%
North Carolina	17	3%
Nevada	18	15%
South Carolina	22	4%
New Mexico	26	6%
Average	**12**	**6%**

"Freedom in the 50 States" ; Mercatus Center,
George Mason University, 2009

(I will point out that I am not virulently anti-union; I am just reporting the facts as they relate to regional economic growth.)

Hispanic Growth

In the past couple decades, the United States had an acute and perpetual shortage of entry-level workers. As the birth rate has declined for non-Hispanic whites, blacks, and Asians, the number of US-born young people available for entry-level work has also declined.

Thus, we have accelerated our reliance on immigrating Hispanics (and they tend to have a higher rate of birth). Therefore, the states that have the highest rates of economic growth are those that have a ready Hispanic labor supply.

A rather amazing 79 percent of Hispanic population growth in the 1980–2010 period has been in the fast-growing states. It is also no surprise that a disproportional percentage of Hispanic population growth is in the states near the Mexican border.

Figure 3.18

Hispanic as Percent of Total Population Change, by Region States with More than 2,000,000 Population 1950-2010							
			Thousands				
	1980		2010		Change 1980-2010		
Region	Total Pop	Total Hispanic	Total Pop	Total Hispanic	Total Change	Hispanic Change	Hispanic Change as % of Total Change
Texas	14,229	2,985	25,146	9,461	10,916	6,475	59%
West Coast	35,254	5,701	58,962	18,785	23,707	13,083	55%
Total Northeast	49,848	2,635	56,768	5,865	6,919	3,229	47%
Total Mid-West	64,924	1,343	74,621	5,110	9,696	3,766	39%
Mountain	4,351	400	7,793	1,397	3,441	996	29%
Total Southeast	44,771	1,280	69,276	7,496	24,504	6,215	25%
Total	213,379	14,347	292,566	48,114	79,186	33,766	43%
Northeast/Mid-West	114,772	3,978	131,389	10,975	16,615	6,995	42%
NE, SE, Mtn. West Coast	98,605	10,366	161,177	37,139	62,568	26,769	43%
% of Total							
Northeast/Mid-West						21%	
NE, SE, Mtn, West Coast						79%	

It is therefore a rather strong position that a major part of the growth of the warmer states is directly correlated with the growth of the Hispanic population.

Other than their climatic differences, proximity to oceans and gulfs and the paucity of unionization, there is one other powerful reason that the fourteen fastest-growing states are what they are: most of the fast-growing states are relatively new.

Social Rigidity

The newness of the fast-growing states means that their infrastructures are far newer, but equally important is their social infrastructure.

The fastest-growing states typically have flexible social structures. In other words, the world of business and finance is not dictated by country-club or social membership or private-school attendance or by family relationships. You don't have to be a non-Hispanic white with ties to the elite and the powerful to succeed in business in these places. These faster-growing states are typically not owned and operated exclusively by old white guys.

In these fast-growing states, you can move up through the social strata by performing well in the world of business and philanthropy. Often, you do not even need wealth to move up the ladder. Good deeds will often do.

This ease of movement in society in these fast-growing states has been particularly advantageous to women, who, in more structured societies in older communities, have been largely shut out.

On balance, the fast-growing states have several powerful tools that are driving their expansion. And none of those tools are anticipated to go away in the next few generations.

The Inertia of Trends

Looking at the key factors, we see a mix of the long lasting effects of technology, government strategic spending, immigration and social factors. While many would take air conditioning and air travel for granted now, their impact on the United States' growth is still ongoing. NASA and Defense spending isn't likely to drastically change in the near future, so we'll likely see their trend continue as well. Time will tell if the faster-growing states will become more socially rigid in the future.

Trends by nature are hard to change, usually because many of them are a bottom-up force with substantial inertia. For example, even if we stopped all Hispanic immigration and enforced an undemocratic China-like one child policy, growth will still continue for decades in the southwest.

World changing technologies like the Internet, mobile computers and renewable energy generation will continue to spread and improve. In the coming years we will more clearly see how this affects our country's (and the rest of the world's) demographics as they gain more inertia with increasing adoption rate.

Conclusion: The Nation is twice of what it was in 1950, however the future growth is now concentrating in the fourteen states in the west and south. There is no single reason but instead eight factors in play and their inertia will be hard to disrupt and change this ongoing Great Divide.

Chapter 4: Manufacturing
The Heart of America

The rumors of the demise of the U.S. manufacturing industry are greatly exaggerated.

—Elon Musk

It may seem odd to devote a whole chapter to manufacturing, but manufacturing has always been the basis for the basic prosperity of our nation—at least until the last few decades.

Until 1970, one-quarter of our total employment was in manufacturing. Then, the Japanese and the Chinese and even Europe began to catch on to the basis of our success. From then on, the percentage of our employment in manufacturing has faded. By 2010, it had fallen to 10.1 percent of our total employment.

Figure 4.1

Manufacturing as % of total Employment United States 1950-2010		
Year	Employment	% of Total
1950	14,884	**24.8%**
1960	16,469	25.0%
1970	20,737	26.3%
1980	21,593	22.2%
1990	21,200	18.0%
2000	19,644	14.3%
2010	14,081	**10.1%**

Source: Bureau of Labor Statistics

That, by the way, does not mean that manufacturing as an industry was failing. In fact, employment from 1970 to 2000 was rather stable. In 2010, in the midst of our recent recession, it did drop, but it is coming back.

Importantly, our productivity in manufacturing has increased rather nicely in recent years after the recessionary setback. In fact, manufacturing output index is substantially above what it was in 1990, increasing from 58.2 in 1990 to 101.5 in 2014.

Figure 4.2

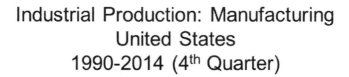

Industrial Production: Manufacturing
United States
1990-2014 (4th Quarter)

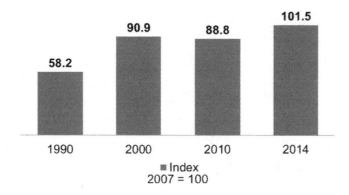

Fortunately, other industries have replaced the manufacturing that we have lost, like high tech, biotech, telecommunications, and others. Better yet, the ones that have replaced manufacturing are very labor-intensive compared to the capital-intensive nature of traditional manufacturing. More on that later.

All US regions have suffered in the manufacturing sector, but the greatest setback has been in the Northeast, which has lost 63 percent of its manufacturing jobs since 1980. The Southeast has lost 39 percent of its manufacturing jobs since 1980, largely as the result of the textile industries going offshore.

Gradually, the Southeast states are replacing those textile jobs with manufacturing jobs in other sectors, like automobiles and aerospace. The balance of the United States has had far less severe losses in the manufacturing sector. On a state-by-state basis, you can see the major declines in the textile and tobacco states, with far lesser declines in the fast-growing states.

Figure 4.3

Change in Employment and Manufacturing Employment Continental United States 1980-2013								
	1980		2013		Change 1980-2013		% Change 1980-2013	
Region	Total	Mfg.	Total	Mfg.	Total	Mfg.	Total	Mfg.
Northeast	22,471	5,380	27,941	1,987	5,470	(3,393)	24%	-63%
Southeast	16,484	3,530	27,153	2,149	10,669	(1,381)	65%	-39%
Midwest	28,464	7,242	37,487	4,672	9,023	(2,570)	32%	-35%
West	14,378	2,748	24,454	1,927	10,076	(821)	70%	-30%
Texas	5,851	1,045	11,036	873	5,185	(172)	89%	-16%
Mountain	2,621	353	4,934	335	2,313	(18)	88%	-5%
United States	90,269	20,298	133,005	11,943	42,736	(8,355)	47%	-41%

Source: Bureau of Labor Statistics

The other state that has taken a big hit is California, which has suffered a 38 percent loss in manufacturing jobs. Back in 1980, California was a hotbed of aerospace and automobile manufacturing, as well as in furniture and apparel. Aerospace and automobile production went to the south (e.g., Mexico), and furniture and apparel manufacturing went mainly to Asia.

Figure 4.4

Total Manufacturing Payroll (000s) 14 Fastest Growing States 1980 and 2013				
State	1980	2013	Change	% Change
Utah	87	117	30	34%
Nevada	19	40	21	111%
Arizona	154	155	1	1%
New Mexico	34	29	(5)	-15%
Washington	308	283	(25)	-8%
Oregon	215	174	(41)	-19%
Colorado	180	132	(48)	-27%
Florida	456	321	(135)	-30%
Georgia	519	355	(164)	-32%
South Carolina	391	224	(167)	-43%
Texas	1,045	873	(172)	-16%
Virginia	413	230	(183)	-44%
North Carolina	820	442	(378)	-46%
California	2,018	1,246	(772)	-38%

Source: Bureau of Labor Statistics

Automobile Manufacturing

Let me turn to the subject of automobile manufacturing, mainly because it has long symbolized American manufacturing and has such a major impact on the economy. In the state of Michigan, the poster child for declining manufacturing jobs (most of them automotive), 265,000 jobs have disappeared since 1990, a meaningful decline of 32 percent.

Figure 4.5

Manufacturing Jobs State of Michigan 1990-2014

Year	No. Jobs	Change from Previous Decade
1990	839,000	n/a
1995	873,000	34,000
2000	896,000	23,000
2005	678,000	(218,000)
2010	473,000	(205,000)
2014	574,500	101,500
Change 1990-2014		-32%

We should note, however, that because of substantial increases in productivity (thanks to robotics), the output of vehicles in Michigan has been increasing steadily since 2010 and continues to account for one out of every five vehicles produced in the United. States.

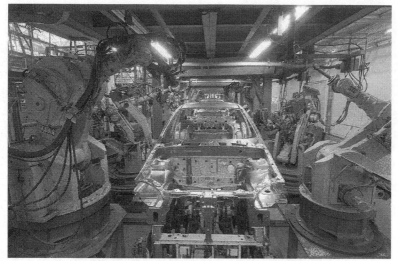
©Mixabest

Figure 4.6

Automobile Production State of Michigan 2007-2014		
Year	Vehicles Produced	% of U.S. Production
2007	2,333,000	22%
2008	1,856,000	21%
2009	1,146,000	20%
2010	1,586,000	20%
2011	1,909,000	22%
2012	2,264,000	22%
2013	2,472,000	23%
2014	2,358,000	21%
Source: Bureau of National Affairs		

The table below shows the changes in automobile-manufacturing employment in the states with significant automobile production. Michigan, Missouri, and Ohio took the big hits, others far smaller ones.

Figure 4.7

Automobile Manufacturing Employment by State United States 1990-2014					
		Employment			
				Change 1990-2014	
Region	State	1990	2014	No.	%
United States		**271,400**	**178,300**	**(93,100)**	**-34.3%**
Midwest	Kentucky	6,100	14,500	8,400	137.7%
Midwest	Michigan	102,000	44,100	(57,900)	-56.8%
Midwest	Missouri	16,500	5,500	(11,000)	-66.7%
Midwest	Ohio	38,300	20,400	(17,900)	-46.7%
Midwest	Indiana	6,100	14,500	8,400	137.7%
Midwest	Tennessee	n/a	10,763	n/a	n/a
Midwest	Illinois	10,030	14,368	4,338	43.3%
Southeast	Alabama	400	11,400	11,000	2750.0%
Southeast	South Carolina	n/a	5,792	n/a	n/a
Southeast	North Carolina	2,774	4,577	1,803	65.0%
Texas	Texas	4,300	11,476	7,176	166.9%
West Coast	California	7,100	2,800	(4,300)	-60.6%
Total Midwest				**(65,662)**	
Total Southeast, Texas & California				**15,679**	

Source: Bureau of Labor Statistics; NAICS 3361

From 2007 to 2011, seventeen automobile-manufacturing plants closed in the United States. All but two were in the Midwest or Northeast. Only two were shuttered in the Southeast.

Figure 4.8

Closures of U.S. Car and Truck Assembly Plants United States 2007-2011				
Date	**Manufacturer**	**State**	**City**	**Region**
2007	Ford	Michigan	Wixon	Midwest
2008	Chrysler	Missouri	St. Louis	Midwest
2009	General Motors	Wisconsin	Janesville	Midwest
2008	General Motors	Ohio	Moraine	Midwest
2009	General Motors	Wisconsin	Janesville	Midwest
2009	General Motors	Michigan	Flint	Midwest
2009	Chrysler	Michigan	Warren	Midwest
2009	General Motors	Michigan	Pontiac	Midwest
2009	General Motors	Tennessee	Spring Hill	Midwest
2009	Chrysler	Missouri	St. Louis	Midwest
2010	Chrysler	Michigan	Warren	Midwest
2010	Ford	Michigan	Wayne	Midwest
2011	Ford	Minnesota	St. Paul	Midwest
2008	Chrysler	Delaware	Newark	Northeast
2009	General Motors	Delaware	Wilmington	Northeast
2007	Ford	Virginia	Norfolk	Southeast
2008	General Motors	Georgia	Doraville	Southeast

No. Midwest	13
No. Northeast	2
No. Southeast	2
Total	17

Source: U.S, Dept. of Commerce, Bureau of Economic Analysis, National Income and Product Accounts, Table 1.25

On a more positive note, since 1980, twenty-six foreign-owned new automobile-manufacturing plants have opened in the United States (plus a few on the Mexican side of our southern border). Of those, fourteen were in the Midwest, and eleven opened in the West and Southeast. Only one opened in Michigan. Virtually all of the plants were of Japanese or Korean ownership.

Figure 4.9

Foreign-Owned Car and Truck Assembly Plants United States 1978-2011					
Region	Year	Company	State	Employees	Capacity
Midwest	1985	Mitsubishi	Illinois	1,950	59,018
Midwest	1989	Subaru	Indiana	2,770	91,581
Midwest	1996	Toyota	Indiana	4,300	300,000
Midwest	2007	Toyota	Indiana	n/a	91,663
Midwest	2008	Honda	Indiana	2,000	200,000
Midwest	1986	Toyota	Kentucky	6,855	500,000
Midwest	1984	Mazda	Michigan	3,200	167,490
Midwest	1982	Honda	Ohio	1,100	800,000
Midwest	1985	Honda	Ohio	2,640	1,180,000
Midwest	1989	Honda	Ohio	2,470	240,000
Midwest	1983	Honda	Tennessee	3,900	550,000
Midwest	1997	Nissan	Tennessee	850	950,000
Midwest	2011	Volkswagen	Tennessee	2,000	150,000
Midwest	1996	Toyota	West Virginia	1,054	414,000
Northeast	1978	Volkswagen	Pennsylvania	(1)	(1)
Southeast	1994	BMW	South Carolina	4,900	170,739
Southeast	2001	Mercedes-Benz	Alabama	3,000	174,000
Southeast	2001	Toyota	Alabama	860	400,000
Southeast	2001	Honda	Alabama	4,000	300,000
Southeast	2003	Nissan	Mississippi	3,400	400,000
Southeast	2005	Hyundai	Alabama	2,700	300,000
Southeast	2010	Toyota	Mississippi	2,000	150,000
Southeast	2010	Kia	Georgia	3,000	360,000
Texas	2003	Toyota	Texas	1,850	200,000
West Coast	1984	NUMMI/Toyoya/GM	California	4,700	342,041
West Coast	2011	Tesla	California	10,000	342,041
Total Midwest				35,089	
Total Southeast				23,860	
Total Texas				1,850	
Total California				10,000	

(1) Built 1.2 million cars between 1978-1989
Source: Congressional Research Service

3D Printing

While the technology was around in the 1980's, in recent years it started becoming cheap enough to no longer need a major company's R&D budget to purchase. Not only are there growing communities of 3D printing hobbyists, there are substantial funds going into further developing 3D printing technology in hopes of creating new kinds of manufacturing. While creating an item could be as simple as pushing a button, to get to that point someone needed to use advanced engineering software to create and prepare the schematics the machine could read.

The jury is still out on how much this development will affect manufacturing production and jobs in the future, however it is something to keep an eye on.

> **Conclusion: The United States continues to be a powerhouse of manufacturing, but it is employing a lot fewer workers, and the workers have to be far more skilled than those of the past. Putting hubcaps on automobiles as they come down the assembly line is no longer a path to a viable retirement.**

Chapter 5: Economic Recoveries
Follow the Money

There was that law of life, so cruel and so just, that one must grow or else pay more for remaining the same.

—Norman Mailer

When I started to do research for this book, my original intent was to show how different US states recover after a recession. Well, I have done that, and I want to show my findings to you. Importantly, the changing nature of economic growth has resulted in major changes in population and employment growth through the years.

For this analysis, I visited the recessions of 1973–1975 and of the early 1980s, as well as the most recent recession.

Recession of 1973–1975

In the recession of 1973–1975, the United States was crippled by a shortage of fuel for cars. Mile-long lines were evident at every gas station. And, of course, the price of fuel escalated according to the law of supply and demand. In addition, the stock market took a big hit. Fortunately, this recession was fairly short.

Officially (in Washington terms), the recession started in November 1973 and ended in March 1975. Peak unemployment was at 9.0 percent, and the gross domestic product from peak to trough declined 3.2 percent.

Recession of 1981–1982

In the recession of the early 1980s, which actually started with (and because of) the Carter administration in 1979, interest rates skyrocketed to 18 percent. As a result, of course, the housing market collapsed (along with the rest of the economy).

Officially, that recession started in July 1981 and ended in November 1982. Peak unemployment was 10.8 percent, and the gross domestic product declined, from peak to trough, 2.7 percent.

As a side note, President Carter's counselors advised him to loosen up the money supply or there would be a huge increase in interest rates. He ignored them, and it took the Reagan administration, with the advice of Arthur Laffer, to correct the situation and move forward with one of the greatest booms in US history.

Recession of 2007–2009

And then, there was the **recent recession**. It started in December 2007 and ended June 2009 (those are Washington's dates, not mine). The unemployment rate peaked at 10.0 percent, and the gross domestic product declined a massive 4.3 percent from peak to trough.

It proved to be one of the most crippling recessions in history because it resulted in a particularly devastating unemployment for the blue-collar, minimum-wage segment of the population. Those with college degrees were not badly wounded, but those with lesser educational levels were hit particularly hard and remain very underemployed today.

The Bureau of Labor Statistics has six different categories of unemployment, rated U-1 through U-6. The official unemployment rate now is below six percent, but the **underemployed** (U-3 to U-6 categories) are at double that percentage.

A summary of the three recessions is shown here:

Figure 5.1

	Official Dates (1)			Peak Unemploy ment	GDP Decline from Peak to Trough
Three Recent Recessions United States					
Basis	Start	Finish	5 Yrs. After Start		
Gas Prices, Stock Mkt. Dip	Nov-73	Mar-75	Nov. 1978	9.0%	-3.2%
High Interest Rates	Jul-81	Nov-82	Nov. 1986	10.8%	-2.7%
Housing Bubble; Financial Collapse	Dec-07	June-2009	Dec. 2012	10.0%	-4.3%

The following table contains a lot of numbers but is probably worth spending a few moments on. The gist of it is that in the successive recessions noted above, rates of recovery (both in terms of population and employment) were different in different states.

In terms of population, if you had the good fortune to live in a state like Texas, North Carolina, Florida, California, or Washington, a very positive population change was evident five years after the start of a recession.

Because this past recession actually lasted more than five years, the population change was not as robust as in past recoveries, but it was still very positive. In the 1974–1975 and early '80s recessions, five years after they began, the populations in the fast-growing states increased more than 10 percent. In the latest recession, it only increased 5.2 percent.

In states like Michigan, Pennsylvania, Ohio, Illinois, and New York, five years after the beginning of the three recessions, the population gains were 3.1 percent after the 1974–75 recession and 0.8 percent after the next two recessions.

The employment statistics followed the same pattern.

In the five fast-growing states, five years after the recessions began, there were substantial employment gains in all three recoveries, with a 20.9 percent job gain in the most recent recovery period.

At the other end of the continuum, in the slow-growing states, the employment changes five years after the recessions began were dismal. In the latest recession, the five states noted here had a net loss of 4.4 percent of jobs at that point.

In almost all cases, their unemployment rates five years after the recent recession began were higher than at the beginning of the recession. Nationally, this past recession evidenced the largest spread in the unemployment rate. Thus, at the beginning of this recession, the unemployment rate in the United States was 4.6 percent, and five years later, it was at 8.0 percent—one of the weakest recoveries in US history.

Even the fast-growing states did not recover as rapidly as in the past in terms of unemployment. Obviously, this recession was far more severe than any of the recessions that I traced going back to the 1960s.

Figure 5.2

History of Economic Recoveries after Recession
Modern Recessions (1973, 1981, 2007)
Selected Fast Growing and Slow Growing States
United States

State	Timeframe	Basis	Official Dates		Timeframe for Analysis			Population Change - 5 Yrs. After Recession Start		Employment Change - 5 Yrs. After Recession Start		Unemployment Rate - 5 Yr. After Recession Start	
			Start	Finish	5 Yrs. After Start	Peak Unempl.	GDP Decline from Peak to Trough	Change	% Change	Change	% Change	Beginning	End
United States	1973-1975	Gas Prices, Stock	Nov-73	Mar-75	Nov 1978	9.0%	-3.2%	10,700,000	5.0%	8,610,000	13.5%	4.8%	6.1%
	Early 1980's	High Interest Rates	Jul-81	Nov-82	July 1986	10.8%	-2.7%	10,660,000	4.6%	7,267,000	9.6%	7.6%	7.0%
	2007-2013	Housing Bubble;	Dec-07	June-2009	Dec 2012	10.0%	-4.3%	12,700,000	4.2%	(2,798,000)	-2.4%	4.6%	8.0%
California, Florida, Texas, North Carolina, Washington	1973-1975	Gas Prices, Stock Mkt. Dip	Nov-73	Mar-75	Nov 1978	9.0%	-3.2%	5,307,501	10.7%	3,578,679	17.6%	7.8%	6.3%
	Early 1980's	High Interest Rates	Jul-81	Nov-82	July 1986	10.8%	-2.7%	6,677,740	11.3%	3,857,177	14.6%	6.6%	7.1%
	2007-2013	Housing Bubble;	Dec-07	June-2009	Dec 2012	10.0%	-4.3%	4,942,317	5.2%	9,287,202	20.9%	5.0%	8.3%
Michigan, Pennsylvania, Ohio, Illinois, New York	1973-1975	Gas Prices, Stock Mkt. Dip	Nov-73	Mar-75	Nov 1978	9.0%	-3.2%	1,832,305	3.1%	(784,091)	-3.0%	4.8%	6.9%
	Early 1980's	High Interest Rates	Jul-81	Nov-82	July 1986	10.8%	-2.7%	200,424	0.8%	1,158,012	4.4%	8.7%	7.6%
	2007-2013	Housing Bubble; Financial Collapse	Dec-07	June-2009	Dec 2012	10.0%	-4.3%	551,558	0.8%	(1,414,790)	-4.4%	5.4%	8.3%

And, of course, all three recessions had massive effects on the price of homes. Most often, the fast-growing states had the highest rate of gain, based on median home prices over the past five years.

Figure 5.3

Five Year Change in Prices Single Family Homes Selected States 2008-2015	
Fast Growing States	**% Change**
Colorado	29.7%
California	17.3%
Texas	20.0%
Nevada	8.7%
Florida	6.2%
Slow Growing States	
Pennsylvania	2.5%
Illinois	4.4%
New Jersey	-5.1%
Delaware	-6.7%
Connecticut	-6.8%
Source: Federal Housing Finance Agency, based on Fanny Mae and Freddie Mac Confirming Conventional Loans	

The change in prices since the recession has varied substantially throughout the nation. In the following table, you can see price changes, or lack thereof, in a bakers' dozen of metropolitan areas.

In the western half of the nation, Denver leads the way, with San Jose in second place. The state of California has led the way to recovery with San Jose (the Silicon Valley) and San Diego at the top of the heap.

The pricing patterns throughout the nation varied substantially, with Seattle and Chicago showing virtually no gains, or worse (even though they both have strong basic economies).

Figure 5.4

Changes in Median Single Family Home Prices ($000) Selected Mettropolitan Areas 2008 - 2015				
Metro Area	2008	2015	2008-2015	% Change
Denver	$ 219	$ 354	$ 135	61.6%
San Jose	$ 668	$ 950	$ 282	42.2%
San Diego	$ 385	$ 543	$ 158	41.0%
San Francisco/East Bay	$ 622	$ 782	$ 160	25.7%
Palm Beach	$ 145	$ 180	$ 35	24.4%
Phoenix	$ 191	$ 216	$ 25	13.1%
D.C./Md./Va.	$ 343	$ 385	$ 42	12.1%
Boston	$ 361	$ 404	$ 43	11.9%
Seattle	$ 357	$ 380	$ 23	6.4%
Milwaukee	$ 212	$ 220	$ 8	3.5%
Philadelphia	$ 231	$ 224	$ (7)	-3.0%
Orlando	$ 209	$ 198	$ (11)	-5.3%
Chicago	$ 245	$ 219	$ (26)	-10.6%
Source: National Association of Realtors				

The Job Market in the Future

The millennials continually worry about their future because they do not see the broad expansion of jobs that they saw when they were in college. They have also been discouraged by the last and longest recession in decades. And we still haven't fully recovered.

After all, our gross national product is still at half the normal rate of recovery and is only now, in 2016, anticipated to move forward at more than a snail's pace. The main problems are threefold: the construction industry is still in the doldrums; people aren't spending like they did in the past on retailing and services; and folks just don't have confidence in the economy or their federal government.

Figure 5.5

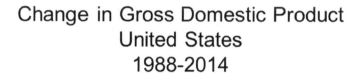

Change in Gross Domestic Product United States 1988-2014

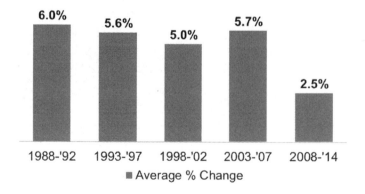

■ Average % Change

Now, having said that, I believe that the future for employment in the next twenty years is really pretty bright—as a result of the aging process.

Figure 5.6

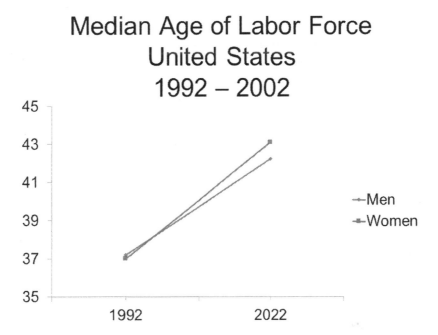

Median Age of Labor Force
United States
1992 – 2002

The median age of the labor force, as shown above, has been continuously increasing, for both men and women. By 2022, the median age for men in the labor force will be over forty-two, and, for women, forty-three.

Now, it is true that folks will be working longer, either because they have to or they want to. They may be perfectly healthy and have no reason to retire. They may change careers after they retire from their first careers. They could become greeters at Walmart.

Take a look at the participation rate anticipated by the Bureau of Labor Statistics. They are showing that the participation rate for those in the sixty-five-to-seventy-four-year-old range will rise 74 percent between 2002 and 2022, increasing from 13.2 percent to 23.0 percent.

And even more astounding is that the seventy-five-and-older crowd is going to double its percentage of participation—from 5.1 percent to 10.5 percent.

Figure 5.7

Participation Rate Civilian Labor Force United States 2002-2022			
Age Group	2002	2022	% Change 2002-2022
25-54	83.3	81.0	-3%
55-64	61.9	67.5	9%
65-74	**13.2**	**23.0**	74%
75 and Older	5.1	10.5	106%
Source: BLS			

Despite the fact that workers are participating later in life, the Bureau of Labor Statistics projects that from 2002 to 2012, twenty-three million men and women will leave the labor force, and from 2012 to 2022, twenty-seven million more will leave, predominantly because they are aged out.

The jobs that they leave will not go away. These workers will need to be replaced, and that is the blessing for the millennials. The majority of physicians, professors, and scientists are over age fifty.

And, as this table shows, the number of entrants into the labor force is greater than the number leaving. But that does not account for the expansion of the total job market. Thus, in the decade from 2012 to 2022, the United States should add another twenty million jobs, and maybe more.

Figure 5.8

Leavers and Stayers Civilian Labor Force United States 2002-2022						
Group	2002-2012			2012-2022		
	Entrants	Leavers	Stayers	Entrants	Leavers	Stayers
Total	33,226	**23,115**	121,749	35,429	**26,954**	128,021
Men	17,742	12,915	64,585	19,723	15,137	67,190
Women	15,484	10,200	57,164	15,706	11,817	60,831
Source: BLS						

Conclusion: If you opt to live in a metropolitan area that has a positive growth path, the number of jobs available will be plentiful as the old folks among us retire to Florida or Palm Springs or Mexico or even San Diego (if they are affluent). Having said that, I note that 85 percent of retirees will stay put in the houses they have been living in for decades.

Chapter 6: The Great State of Texas
Capitalism Trumps All

Texas, O Texas! your freeborn single star,
Sends out its radiance to nations near and far,
Emblem of Freedom! it set our hearts aglow,
With thoughts of San Jacinto and glorious Alamo.

—Texas State Song

I don't think I'd want to live in Texas, but you certainly can't fault its unbridled capitalism and spirit. It is the heart of the nation's capitalism, and God help anyone who tries to get in the way. It is a property-rights state and has an abiding distaste for unions.

This philosophy is, of course, the direct opposite of that of California, and, as a result, the state of Texas completely ignored the most recent recession and has come roaring forward with its monstrous job machine.

Texas elected officials always ask themselves: "Is it good for business?"California' elected officials ask: "Is it good for the unions?"

The unemployment rate in Texas was continuously below that of the rest of the nation throughout the recession and bounced back rapidly. Its unemployment rate now is 5.1 percent.

Figure 6.1

Total Employment State of Texas June 2004 - June 2014		
Year	Total	Change
2004	10,348,140	n/a
2005	10,543,220	195,080
2006	10,724,069	180,849
2007	10,883,663	159,594
2008	11,068,906	185,243
2009	11,067,500	(1,406)
2010	11,284,197	216,697
2011	11,468,192	183,995
2012	11,725,523	257,331
2013	11,997,145	271,622
2014	12,329,644	332,499

Source: Bureau of Labor Statistics

Just as an aside, the feds now say that full employment is defined as 6 percent unemployment. A few years ago, it was 5 percent, and before that, 4 percent. The Full-Employment Act was passed in 1946.

Figure 6.2

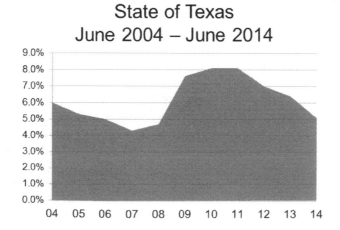

Looking at the five key industries that drive the Texas economy—construction; manufacturing; education and health services; trade, transportation, and utilities; and professional and business services—all moved through the recession relatively unscathed. Those industries that experienced weakness in the recession have bounced back, and every one except manufacturing is above what it was ten years ago. And, manufacturing itself is dead level with ten years ago—a mighty achievement when you look at what has happened to manufacturing in other states.

Texas governors brag about the Texas job machine. They have every right to do so. And, frankly, they don't have to take out ads in California, Illinois, and Pennsylvania to make their case.

Figure 6.3

Economic Drivers State of Texas June 2004-June 2014					
Year	Construction	Mfg.	Educaton & Health Services	Trade, Transport, Utilities	Prof. & Business Services
2004	541	889	1,146	1,942	1,101
2005	561	894	1,180	1,988	1,151
2006	605	926	1,214	2,046	1,238
2007	648	937	1,255	2,114	1,303
2008	676	929	1,287	2,148	1,342
2009	598	832	1,335	2,056	1,247
2010	564	810	1,383	2,052	1,272
2011	561	834	1,412	2,106	1,338
2012	583	864	1,443	2,176	1,409
2013	614	872	1,481	2,240	1,456
2014	634	885	1,529	2,333	1,521

Source: Bureau of Labor Statistics

As you might suspect, population follows jobs. The state of Texas has experienced remarkable population growth since the 1950s, with massive population gains in virtually every decade. What is particularly notable is the growth since the 1980s and the stunning population gain in the past decade. From 2000 to 2010, the state added more than four million residents.

Figure 6.4

Population Change State of Texas 1940-2010		
Year	Population	Change from Previous Decade
1940	6,414,824	n/a
1950	7,711,194	1,296,370
1960	9,579,677	1,868,483
1970	11,196,730	1,617,053
1980	14,229,191	3,032,461
1990	16,986,510	2,757,319
2000	20,851,820	3,865,310
2010	25,145,561	4,293,741

About half of the growth is the result of more people being born than dying. The balance of the growth is from migration. And the migration is a balance between domestic migration and international migration. That picture has changed very little in the past twenty years.

Figure 6.5

Population - Components of Change State of Texas 1990-2010		
Source of Change	1990-1999	2000-2010
Natural Increase		
Births	3,025,567	3,568,617
Deaths	1,254,005	1,444,493
Net Natural Increase	**1,771,562**	**2,124,124**
Migation		
Domestic	569,957	848,702
International	715,420	957,656
Total Migration	**1,285,377**	**1,806,358**
Total Population Change	**3,056,939**	**3,930,482**
% of Total		
Net Natural Increase	58%	54%
Domestic Migration	19%	22%
International Migration	23%	24%
Total	100%	100%

In terms of ethnicity, and looking into the future, the Texas Hispanic population is projected to add fourteen million people, the Asian (and other) almost six million, and the black population a mere 1.7 million. The non-Hispanic white population will barely add 7 percent to its base—less than one million.

These projections, through 2040 are based on the assumption that net migration will be equal to that of the 2000 to 2010 period.

Figure 6.6

Projected Ethnicity State of Texas 2010-2040				
Ethnicity	2010	2040	Change	% Change
Non-Hispanic White	11,397,345	12,194,151	796,806	7%
Black	2,886,825	4,653,725	1,766,900	61%
Hispanic	9,460,921	23,514,974	14,054,053	149%
Asian & Other	1,400,470	7,283,548	5,883,078	420%
Total	25,145,561	47,646,398	22,500,837	89%

Note: Assumes Net Migration Equal to 2000-2010
Source: Hobby Center for the Study of Texas at Rice University

Thus, in the 2010–2040 period, 62 percent of the total population change will be Hispanic, 26 percent Asian (and other), 8 percent black, and a very meager 4 percent non-Hispanic white. Slowly but surely, the Hispanics are reclaiming Texas for themselves. Thus, the Treaty of Guadalupe Hidalgo, signed in 1846, may be moot.

Texas has made major strides in education in the past twenty years. Historically, it has been a laggard in K-12 education, particularly for minorities. Since 1990, there has been a major improvement in both high-school and college attendance, with particular advances in the Hispanic and black populations.

The black population has seen high-school achievement advance from 66 percent to 86 percent and college advancement from 12 percent to 20 percent.

The Hispanic population, similarly, has seen its high-school advancement rise from 45 percent to 60 percent and college from 7 percent to 12 percent.

Obviously, there is a long way to go for the blacks and Hispanics to achieve parity with non-Hispanic whites and the Asian population, but they are making progress.

Figure 6.7

Education Levels State of Texas 1990-2010				
	High School & Higher		College & Higher	
Category	1990	2010	1990	2010
Non-Hispanic White	82%	92%	25%	34%
Black	66%	86%	12%	20%
Hispanic	45%	60%	7%	12%
Asian & Other	79%	87%	41%	46%

Source: Hobby Center for the Study of Texas at Rice University

The Five Major Metropolitan Areas

Five metropolitan areas comprise two-thirds of the population of Texas: Houston, Dallas/Fort Worth, Austin, San Antonio, and El Paso.

Dallas/Fort Worth and Houston are battling it out for first place in the population competition; they are both in the range of six million in population. Well behind them are San Antonio, Austin, and El Paso, in that order. Most have doubled or nearly doubled their populations in the past thirty years, except El Paso, which just seems to mosey along. In total, Texas has added 77 percent to its population base in the 1980–2010 time frame. Big numbers! Big state!

Figure 6.8

Population Change Major Metropolitan Areas Texas 1980-2010				
Metropolitan Area	1980	2010	Change	Change %
Big Five				
Dallas/Ft. Worth	3,017,230	6,426,214	3,408,984	113%
Houston	3,017,230	5,920,416	2,903,186	96%
San Antonio	1,124,819	2,142,508	1,017,689	90%
Austin	585051	1,716,289	1,131,238	193%
El Paso	480,000	800,647	320,647	67%
Other Counties	13,749,191	24,344,914	10,595,723	77%
Texas	**14,229,191**	**25,145,561**	**10,916,370**	**77%**

As you look at the proportional share of the population gains from 1980 to 2010, 80 percent of them were in those five major metropolitan areas. It is part of the urbanization of Texas. In 2010, Dallas and Houston accounted for 50 percent of the population but 58 percent of the change in that thirty-year period.

Figure 6.9

Share of the Change Major Metropolitan Areas Texas 1980-2010			
Metropolitan Area	**1980**	**2010**	**% of Change**
Austin	4%	7%	10%
Dallas/Ft. Worth	21%	26%	31%
Houston	21%	24%	27%
San Antonio	8%	9%	9%
El Paso	3%	3%	3%
Big Five	**58%**	**68%**	**80%**
Other Counties	42%	32%	20%
Texas	**100%**	**100%**	**100%**

Dallas/Fort Worth

With a population bulging over six million, Dallas/Fort Worth, if it were a state, would be the fifteenth-largest in the nation, about the same size as Massachusetts. The major difference there is that Dallas/Fort Worth will keep on growing, but Massachusetts will just keep moving along as it has been.

In this nation, there are six major distribution centers, all anchored by enormous airports: Atlanta, New York, Chicago, Denver, Los Angeles, and Dallas/Fort Worth. All six have more than twenty-five million enplanements annually (i.e., the number of people boarding). Dallas/Fort Worth is solidly in fourth place, with twenty-eight million enplanements annually. Just for the record, that's seventy-five thousand passengers per day.

Dallas/Fort Worth is a business metro. It is home to more than a hundred thousand businesses and has fifteen hundred corporate headquarters. It ranks fourth in the nation in *Fortune* magazine's list of corporate headquarters. Dallas is inevitably rated among the very best places in the nation to do business and start a business.

It has a remarkable number of world-class cultural and recreational structures, including AT&T Stadium (where the Dallas Cowboys play), American Airlines Arena, the Meyerson Symphony Center, Nasher Sculpture Center, and the Perot Museum of Nature and Science. There appears to be an endless number of billionaires in Dallas who just love to have their names on buildings.

Houston

Make no mistake; there is only one Houston in the world. That may be a good thing. It is the city with no zoning and, as far as I can tell, no rules about anything. It is solidly the oil and gas capital of the nation and may be near the top in health-care services.

It is hot, humid, often smelly, and downright inhospitable. And it is all business. It is number four in the nation in terms of gross domestic product (only New York, Los Angeles and Chicago are ahead of it).

©Taurus Auriga

It is the energy capital of the world. Half of the economic activity in the metropolitan area is linked to oil and gas production and exploration. Six of the top twenty employers there are energy related, including Exxon, Shell, and Chevron. It has the second-highest concentration of engineers in the nation, second only to the Silicon Valley. There are thirty-seven hundred energy-related firms in the metropolitan area.

©Larry D. Moore

Health services also abound in Houston. There are six major hospitals in Houston and a health-care system that employs almost three hundred thousand.

It also has an amazing selection of cheap housing. I don't know how they do it, but they produce new homes for prices that make you wonder how they are made. Maybe with 3-D printers.

It is the third most humid city in the nation, upstaged by only New Orleans and Jacksonville. But all six million folks who live there suffer through, because it is employment central.

Austin

Austin is a delightful blend of academics and government. Both industries are remarkably resilient to downturns in the economy.

Anchoring the community is the University of Texas at Austin, with fifty thousand students and a faculty and staff of twenty-four thousand. It is ranked twelfth in the nation of all the large schools in a recent Kiplinger Report.

State government is the other mega player, with seventy thousand employees—and that does not include lobbyists or other hangers-on. Austin is the state capital, after all.

UT Austin has become a focal point for a wide range of scientific and professional business services that rely on the brainpower at the university. There are some eighty thousand-plus people engaged in information, scientific, and technical services in the metro.

Austin is probably the most attractive of all the big metros in Texas.

San Antonio

San Antonio matches Austin in terms of employment. Both have nine hundred thousand payroll jobs. These do not include jobs in the military, which plays a major role in the San Antonio economy. Uniformed personnel total more than forty thousand. And there are fifty-five thousand retired military living there. Medical services plays a large role in the military in San Antonio, and the metro is home to the USAF School of Aerospace Medicine.

Figure 6.10

	Military Operations San Antonio 2013							
	Uniformed Active							
Base	Army	Navy	Marine	Air Force	Total	Reserve	Civilian	Total
Brooks	7	-	-	-	7	-	33	40
Jt. Base	9,489	3,918	164	21,332	34,903	5,645	21,552	62,100
Kelly	-	4		14	18	171	578	767
Total	9,496	3,922	164	21,346	34,928	5,816	22,163	62,907

Source: U.S. DOD, Base Structure Report, 2013

Professional, science, and technical services and information systems, along with health care, employ yet another 250,000.

Another hundred thousand-plus are employed in the tourism sector. San Antonio has a strong draw as a vacation destination because of its River Walk and history and not-so-bad weather.

El Paso

Located at the far west end of Texas, looking at Ciudad Juárez across the border, the sleepy town of El Paso continues to grow by about ten thousand per year.

Like San Antonio, it has a military presence. Fort Bliss has 33,000 personnel on its 122,000 acres.

El Paso serves as Ciudad Juárez's shopping center and, for many, its health care. At one time, El Paso was a large apparel manufacturing center, particularly for jeans, but that went offshore some time ago. Of the three hundred thousand jobs in El Paso, only eighteen thousand are in manufacturing.

Ciudad Juárez, with its crime infestation, has cast a pall over El Paso. The Department of State assesses crime as "critical" in Juárez. In 2013, 530 people were murdered there. This is a substantial improvement, however, over the 730 murders reported in 2012 and the 1,900 reported in 2011. A significant majority of homicides in that city are drug-cartel related; however, there have been cases in which innocent people were caught in the line of fire or mistakenly targeted.

As a major drug-trafficking corridor, the state of Chihuahua has been contested by two major transnational criminal organizations (TCOs) for years. With more availability of drugs in Juárez, drug use has also increased locally. Carjackings are also a cottage industry.

El Paso is just a barrel of fun.

Conclusion: Texas is lean, mean, and supreme in its long-term plan to become the number-one center of capitalism in the United States, casting its shadow over the other forty-nine. "Right to work" is an inherent part of the DNA of Texas. And recessions are anathema. Just won't be tolerated.

Chapter 7: California
A State of Mind

California is a state of mind, but it is also a state of great production. If it were a nation (and some folks are working on that), it would be the sixth largest nation in the world in terms of gross domestic production, just behind United Kingdom. The way things are going in Europe, the Golden State might be in fifth or even fourth place before long. (Just for bragging rights, Texas is number thirteen.)

Figure 7.1

GDP ($billions) Top Ten Nations and California 2016		
Rank	Nation	GNP
1	United States	$ 18,558,130
2	China	$ 11,383,030
3	Japan	$ 4,412,600
4	Germany	$ 3,467,780
5	United Kingdom	$ 2,760,960
6	California	$ 2,564,000
7	France	$ 2,464,790
8	India	$ 2,288,720
9	Italy	$ 1,848,690
10	Brazil	$ 1,534,780

I have put together a good-and-bad report card for California. I don't know if I covered all the bases, but probably most:

Figure 7.2

What's Good and Bad About California	
Good	**Bad**
Great weather	Remarkably anti-business
On the Ocean	Ruinous tax structure
Proximity to Mexico & Canada	Environmental insanity
Gateway to the Far East	Mis-guided electorate
6 Great Universities	An occasional earthquake
Highly motivated work force	No respect for property rights
Exceptional ports	Warped Coastal Commission
Center of "brain" industries	Permanent housing shortage near Coast
Continual population growth	High price of housing
Strong Hispanic in-migration	Unmanageable budget
Remarkable selection of recreational choicee	Tsunami candidate
A multitude of strong recession-proof industries	Brain-dead bureaucracy
Heart of venture capital expenditures	PETA
Minimal social rigidity	

What generally stands out as the greatness of the state is its remarkable selection of good jobs, growing industries, import/export businesses, and an entrepreneurial brain trust.

What is remarkable, therefore, is that its antibusiness attitude, a far-left legislature, off-base environmentalists, inferior K-12 school system, and unfriendly tax structure have not dragged the state down into oblivion. California, in every survey, is ranked forty-ninth or last in probusiness attitude. And yet, it prospers.

In the words attributed to Count Leopold Berchtold of Austria, "The situation is hopeless, but not serious."

California may be unmanageable with its current convoluted government structure, but it will, nonetheless, continue to grow. The demise of a viable

California has been long predicted, but the waterfront state just keeps on growing.

In most decades, the state adds three to four million people (more than the population of Orange County Ca.). Its population gains ebb and flow based on the national economy. During the Reagan years, California shared in the good times and added more than six hundred thousand in population each year in the 1980s. Then, during the Clinton years, when the nation added twenty-two million jobs and had no federal debt, the state added more than four hundred thousand people annually.

In the 2000–2010 decade, the massive recession that started in 2007 and lasted into the following decade caused a substantial slowdown in population growth in California: it only added about 3.2 million residents. By way of comparison, that is more than all nineteen of the states in the Midwest combined added in the same period.

Figure 7.3

California Population 1950-2010			
Year	Population	Change from Last Decade	Annual Change from Last Decade
1950	10,586,223	n/a	n/a
1960	15,863,000	5,276,777	527,678
1970	20,039,000	4,176,000	417,600
1980	23,667,902	3,628,902	362,890
1990	29,944,000	6,276,098	627,610
2000	34,088,000	4,144,000	414,400
2010	37,253,956	3,165,956	316,596

Source: California Department of Finance

California grows as a result of both natural increase (births over deaths) and migration (international and from within the States). Typically, when the economy is booming, more immigration occurs. Every decade is decidedly different. Thus, in the 1960s, immigration accounted for 60 percent of growth compared to 1990 and 2000, when immigration accounted for less than half of population gain.

Importantly, since 1990, natural increase has been relatively stable and approaching three hundred thousand annually. From 1980 through 2000, immigration was typically three hundred thousand annually.

In 2010, largely due to the recession, immigration flatlined, and California's total population gain in 2010 was a meager 232,000. Since then, it has picked up again. In 2014, the natural increase was 243,000 and the immigration 118,000, for a total gain of 335,000 (more like normalcy).

Figure 7.4

Population Component of Change (000) California 1950-2014						
Year	Total Change	Natural Increase	Births	Deaths	Migration	% of Change from Migration
1950	306	145	244	99	161	53%
1960	575	237	372	135	338	59%
1970	294	193	358	165	101	34%
1980	525	210	390	180	315	60%
1990	686	381	594	213	305	44%
2000	582	298	525	228	284	49%
2010	232	283	516	233	-51	-22%
2014	335	243	497	254	118	35%

Source: California Department of Finance

It will come as no surprise to you that the guiding force behind California's population growth is the expansion of the Hispanic population, and, to a lesser degree, the Asian population. In the 1980–2010 census reports, the state gained 13.6 million in population. Of that total, 70 percent was Hispanic growth, and Asian, 27 percent. The non-Hispanic whites (i.e., "gringos") had a 7 percent decline as a percent of change. From a pure, raw-numbers standpoint, of the 13.6 million population gain in the state, 9.5 million was Hispanic.

The other category that has had a major uptick is "other." The growth of "other" is a result of assimilation and more people identifying themselves as something other than pure black, Hispanic, or Asian. That category will continue to increase dramatically in future years.

Figure 7.5

Ethnicity of Population California 1980-2010							
	1980		2010		Change		
Ethnicity	Population	Percent	Population	Percent	Population	Percent	% of Change
Non-Hispanic White	15,850,775	67.0%	14,956,253	63.2%	(894,522)	-6%	-6.6%
Hispanic	4,541,300	19.2%	14,013,719	59.2%	9,472,419	209%	69.7%
Asian	1,242,157	5.2%	4,861,007	20.5%	3,618,850	291%	26.6%
Black	1,784,086	7.5%	2,299,072	9.7%	514,986	29%	3.8%
Other	249,584	1.1%	1,123,905	4.7%	874,321	350%	6.4%
Total	23,667,902	100.0%	37,253,956	157.4%	13,586,054	57%	100.0%

California's Demographic Research Department (part of the Department of Finance) recently released its projections for the year 2040, about a quarter century from now. It does not foresee any discernable changes from the past thirty years.

DOF is projecting 71 percent of the population growth between 2010 and 2040 to be Hispanic and 16 percent Asian. Gringos will just about hold their own unless the millennials decide that it is OK to have large families again. Thus, of the 10.4 million gain in the 2010–2014 period, 96 percent of it is something other than non-Hispanic white.

Perhaps the most important thing is that DOF is projecting an annual average population gain of 350,000. I wonder if anybody in the California government structure is trying to figure out where we are going to put another ten million people and how wide the highways have to be to accommodate them. I doubt if the San Joaquin Valley train to nowhere that is being funded is anticipated to provide the predominant transportation for the ten million newcomers.

Figure 7.6

Ethnicity of Population California 2010-2040							
	2010		2040		Change		
Ethnicity	Population	Percent	Population	Percent	Population	Percent	% of Change
Non-Hispanic White	14,956,253	40.1%	14,342,695	38.5%	(613,558)	-1.6%	-6.1%
Hispanic	14,013,719	37.6%	21,475,903	57.6%	7,462,184	20.0%	74.8%
Asian	4,861,007	13.0%	6,905,370	18.5%	2,044,363	5.5%	20.5%
Black	2,299,072	6.2%	2,357,738	6.3%	58,666	0.2%	0.6%
Other	1,123,905	3.0%	2,151,534	5.8%	1,027,629	2.8%	10.3%
Total	37,253,956	100.0%	47,233,240	126.8%	9,979,284	26.8%	100.0%

Source: California Department of Finance, Demographic Section

Some folks think there are six Californias. I only know of four: the Bay Area (including Sacramento); Southern California; the Central Valley (i.e., San Joaquin Valley); and everywhere else. The "everywhere else" counties (thirty-one of the fifty-eight) account for only 8 percent of the state's population. They are projected to maintain that percentage.

Thus, I shall concentrate on the twenty-seven counties that contain 92 percent of California's population (and, therefore, 92 percent of future growth).

Admittedly, the thirty-one counties that I won't discuss contain some of the most beautiful scenery in the state, but, economically speaking, they are not an important part of the state's revenue stream.

Figure 7.7

Percent of Population by Area California

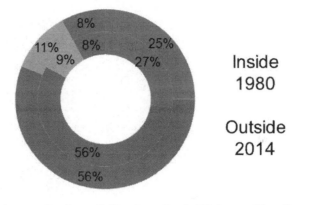

■ Bay Area ■ Southern California ■ Central Valley ■ Other Counties

The state has recently released its population estimates for 2014. In the table below, we can look at the changes since the 1980 census. The state has added 14.5 million people. Of the 14.5 million, more than half wound up in Southern California, the six-county region that includes Los Angeles, Orange, San Diego, Riverside, San Bernardino, and Ventura Counties. That region alone added more than 8.1 million in population over the 1980–2014 time frame.

The Bay Area also had a healthy growth path, adding 3.3 million people in that thirty-year time frame. And the steaming Central Valley doubled in size and now has a population of four million.

Figure 7.8

Population by Sector of States California 1980-2014				
			Change	
Area	1980	2014	No.	%
Bay Area	6,304,100	9,629,759	3,325,659	53%
Southern California	13,422,600	21,558,753	8,136,153	61%
Central Valley	2,062,400	4,102,351	2,039,951	99%
Other Counties	1,992,900	3,049,211	1,056,311	53%
Total State	23,782,000	38,340,074	14,558,074	61%

Source: California Dept. of Finance

Looking out to the future, not much is expected to change. In fact, almost nothing is expected to change except that the Central Valley is anticipated grow a little more. And it will.

Figure 7.9

Percent of Population by Area California 2014-2040		
Area	2014	2040
Bay Area	25%	24%
Southern California	56%	54%
Central Valley	11%	14%
Other Counties	8%	8%
Total State	100%	100%

Source: California Dept. of Finance

During the next quarter century, Southern California is projected to add another 4.2 million people, the Central Valley, 2.5 million, and the Bay Area a fairly modest 1.8 million.

Figure 7.10

Population Projections by Sector of State California 2014-2040				
			Change	
Area	2014	2040	No.	%
Bay Area	9,629,759	11,413,020	1,783,261	19%
Southern California	21,558,753	25,724,732	4,165,979	19%
Central Valley	4,102,351	6,660,720	2,558,369	62%
Other Counties	3,049,211	3,891,714	842,503	28%
Total State	38,340,074	47,690,186	9,350,112	24%

The median age in California is 35.2, slightly below that of the nation. The important thing to note in the table below is the differential between the ages of the Hispanic population and those of the non-Hispanic white population.

The median age increase of the non-Hispanic white population is somewhat startling, increasing from 31.9 to 44.6 years of age between the 1980 and 2010 censuses. That's a 40 percent increase.

The black population also increased its median age substantially. The median age of the Asian population in California was not reported in the 1980 census.

Figure 7.11

Median Age California 1980-2010			
Ethnicity	1980	2010	Change
Non-Hispanic White	31.9	44.6	12.7
Hispanic	22.3	27.1	4.8
Asian	n/a	37.8	n/a
Black	25.7	35.6	9.9
Total	29.9	35.2	5.3

In the 2010 census, Hispanic households have substantially more occupants than the household sizes in the other ethnic categories. In fact, Hispanic households, both owner- and renter-occupied, have almost twice the number of residents than the households of non-Hispanic whites.

And, uniformly, renter-occupied housing has fewer residents per unit than owner-occupied homes in all ethnic categories. This is because owner-occupied units have more bedrooms than renter-occupied units.

Figure 7.12

Average Household Size by Tenure and Ethnicity California 2010		
Tenure	**Owner Occupied**	**Renter Occupied**
Non-Hispanic White	2.46	2.16
Hispanic	4.09	3.81
Asian	3.34	2.75
Black	2.77	2.48

Below shows the number of births in the state of California for 2000 and 2010, with the state's projections for 2020. It is this projection that leads to the future ethnic mix I described earlier in the chapter.

Figure 7.13

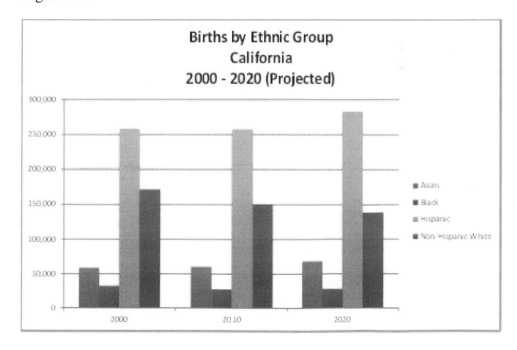

The Job Market in California

California has perpetually been a job machine, but it faltered in this past recession. Now, however, it is coming back. In the past five years, the state has gained almost 1.8 million jobs.

Figure 7.14

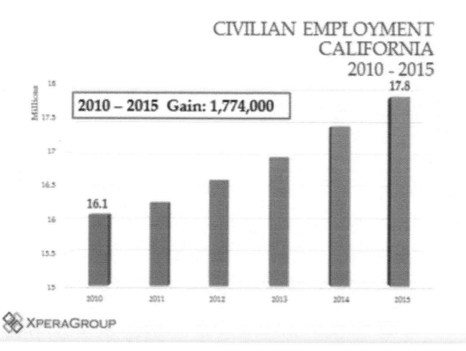

With jobs on the upswing, the unemployment rate declined from a most unacceptable 11 percent in 2011 to a far more palatable 5.9 percent at the end of 2015. Note that the spread against the US rate has narrowed in the past few years. In fact, it has been cut in half.

Figure 7.15

Year	California	United States	Spread
Unemployment Rate California and United States 2010-2015			
2009	12.1%	9.3%	2.8%
2010	12.1%	9.6%	2.5%
2011	11.0%	8.9%	2.1%
2012	9.5%	8.1%	1.4%
2013	8.2%	6.8%	1.4%
2014	7.1%	5.6%	1.5%
2015	5.9%	5.0%	0.9%

Source: Bureau of Labor Statistics

Basically, all the major industry segments that drive the California economy have rebounded, although the construction industry has not regained its full strength by any measure. In August 2007, the California construction industry had 920,000 jobs and now has two-thirds that many.

The three major economic drivers, professional and business services, educational and health services, and leisure and hospitality, have added 18.3 percent, 16.5 percent, and 15.5 percent respectively in the past four years. That's a gain of almost a million jobs in those three industries.

Figure 7.16

Payroll Employment, Major Industries California 2010-2014 (End of Year)				
Industry	2010	2014	Change	% Change
Professional & Business Services	2,102,000	2,486,000	**384,000**	18.3%
Educational & Health Services	2,071,000	2,412,000	**341,000**	16.5%
Leisure & Hospitality	1,516,000	1,751,000	**235,000**	15.5%
Construction	553,000	680,000	127,000	23.0%
Information	429,000	477,000	48,000	11.2%
Financial Activities	762,000	779,000	17,000	2.2%
Manufacturing	1,243,000	1,254,000	11,000	0.9%
Government	2,425,000	2,373,000	(52,000)	-2.1%

Source: California Employment Development Department

Though projections are merely statistical and are inevitably based on history, it is my contention that the state will continue to prosper and most likely will add more than three hundred thousand jobs in this decade.

Please note that the population is projected to grow by three hundred thousand each year, which should mean that the unemployment rate will decline and that more people who want to work full time can do so.

Those projections are very pleasant—but remember that IBM once projected the total market for their mainframes at five.

The Four Sectors of California

The Bay Area

By my definition, the Bay Area consists of nine counties plus the Sacramento area. The nine counties include San Francisco, San Mateo, Alameda, Contra Costa, Santa Clara, and the suburban counties of Napa, Santa Rosa, Solano, and Marin.

The Sacramento metropolitan area consists of four counties: Sacramento, Placer, Yolo, and Eldorado. Sacramento is the heart of the employment scene. The other three are suburbs.

Anchored by UC Berkeley and Stanford, the Bay Area has become the nation's greatest mecca for software and electronic innovation. Without belaboring the situation, Apple, Google, Yahoo, Salesforce, Oracle, Intel, and dozens of other mega masters of our electronic universe would not be there if it were not for their connections with Stanford and UC Berkeley.

Larry Summers, former US Treasury head and now a Silicon Valley advisor, was recently asked by *Fortune* magazine: "Do you sense the air is different in the Silicon Valley?" His answer: "There is an enormous rejection of constraints."

That man isn't lovable, but he is correct. The Silicon Valley (and its junior partner, San Diego County) does not accept constraints. It creates tomorrow's world by hiring the brainiest entrepreneurial young professionals and allows them to become megamillionaires by taking off the constraints that have ruined such industries as automobile manufacturing.

Much of the exponential expansion of the high-tech industries would not be possible without venture capital. The explosion of available venture capital is unprecedented. It is high-risk capital with the potential for very substantial rewards. The venture-capital industry is centered in Menlo Park near Stanford University (on the vaunted Sand Hill Road).

If the Silicon Valley has one flaw, it is that it is heavily male-dominated, with few women in managerial positions. It is working to correct that imbalance, but equality in the Silicon Valley is a long way away.

The one other thing that makes the Bay Area stand out is the City of San Francisco. It does have its share of unbalanced people, but it is a real city, the only one in the state of California. It is a world-class city because it combines a massive educated workforce with a highly livable (though a little expensive) environment. And, to top that, its wealth has allowed it to create remarkable theaters and museums and sports venues.

And its selection of clothing and accessories within a centralized core area is unmatched in California and maybe anywhere west of the Mississippi. It is the epitome of 24/7/365.

It also has a highly efficient and likeable transportation system that allows folks to live in the suburbs and work downtown without getting in their cars.

I also include Sacramento within the Bay Area because it is almost commutable. Sacramento is the seat of California's government, but, unlike the Bay Area, it is uncreative, stodgy, and moves along at a glacial pace. It's sort of like a wart that won't go away. It really doesn't relate at all to the Bay Area and creates nothing but legislation with unintended consequences. It is the philosophical antithesis of the Bay Area. Its sole redeeming feature is its proximity to Lake Tahoe and good skiing.

Southern California

Inevitably referred to as "the land of the fruits and nuts," Southern California is an interesting environment. It is a conglomerate of a multitude of cities and counties, each with its own benefits and foibles.

There are six counties in Southern California: Los Angeles, Orange, Riverside, San Bernardino, Ventura, and San Diego. Ventura really doesn't have its own character—it's really a minor western suburb of Los Angeles.

Los Angeles

Los Angeles County is routinely criticized because it is a large, unstructured blob with eighty-eight cities and another eighty unincorporated communities. It is a world of its own. It is so large and so diverse that it defies description. It has the largest port in the nation; is the heart of the world of movies and television. It has an enormous import/export business and, basically, is a nation of ten million people unto itself.

Los Angeles is the number-one import/export port in the United States. The total value of two-way trade handled at the Los Angeles Port District is approximately $400 billion annually.

It also has a remarkable mix of ethnicities speaking a myriad of tongues. The county is 27 percent non-Hispanic white, 48 percent Hispanic, 15 percent Asian, and 9 percent black. Some two hundred-plus languages are spoken there.

It has 113 accredited colleges, not the least of which are UCLA and USC, and it has a highly generous group of folks who have funded some of the finest sports, museums, and music and entertainment venues in the world.

And, to its credit, it is in the midst of developing a world-class people-moving transportation system, including buses and trolleys and subways. Within twenty years, it will be possible to reach all the major employment centers with rapid transit.

Downtown Los Angeles had basically no residential base ten years ago. Since then, the downtown population has doubled as dozens of new rental and for-sale product has been built. In addition, a substantial number of obsolete office structures have been converted to apartments and condominiums. And it's just starting. There are more than 100 projects underway in downtown Los Angeles.

Los Angeles County is so big and complex that it is indescribable, so I'll stop trying to describe it.

Orange County

Orange County is a little more manageable from a description standpoint. It is a business county, clear and simple. It is a financial, headquarters, and legal hub that supports its three million in population, mostly in silicone-enhanced, superficial style.

Its major claim to fame is Disneyland—an entertainment scene that has fostered an entire realm of family fun and an enormous tourism industry. Disneyland attendance is estimated at sixteen million annually. It also has two rather decent universities: University of California at Irvine and Chapman University.

There are really two Orange Counties: the elitist south and the multiethnic north. The elitist south is anchored by the Irvine Company holdings and several other major, master-planned communities that can be described as "plastic." They are inhabited by a blend of non-Hispanic whites and Asians, both of which are tied to the south county's superb school system. It is superb because the students are superb. SAT scores and university admissions are the primary topics of discussion in most families here.

The nonelitist north of the county contains a blend of predominantly Hispanic and Asian communities, many of them engaged in small businesses that serve the local residents.

Like Los Angeles County, Orange County does have a wonderful collection of entertainment, sports, cultural, and recreation venues and some rather nice beaches and marinas.

Politically, the county leans a little to the right. Genghis Khan might be happy here.

Riverside and San Bernardino Counties ("The Inland Empire")

Two counties that are joined at the hip and serve as bedroom communities for the working folk of the counties of Orange, Los Angeles, and, occasionally, San Diego are Riverside and San Bernardino Counties, otherwise known as the Inland Empire.

The two counties don't really have much going for them except their proximity to Orange and Los Angeles Counties. They are virtually void of character, charm, and attitude. They are a series of suburban communities that are often very livable but without downtowns or other reasons to exist.

With a few exceptions, neither county has attracted base employment even though the land is much cheaper there than in Orange and Los Angeles counties. If you really enjoy two-hour commutes to work, then the Inland Empire is the place for you.

Riverside County does have the Palm Springs area, but, that, too, is a crashing bore unless you are gay or into pottery throwing (or both). It has a few nice resorts and golf courses, but that's about it. Oh, yes, it is unbearably hot in the summer. People living there are really wrinkled.

And the northern part of San Bernardino County does have lovely forests and hiking and boating and skiing, so it's not all bad. Places like Big Bear Lake and Lake Arrowhead come to mind.

There's really not much else to say about the two counties except that they are growing. I guess that is positive.

San Diego County

San Diego County is an interesting place. It is closely associated with Tijuana-centered Baja California. Between the two metropolises, there are almost five million people. North of the border is a nice community of three million people.

This county has an exceptionally broad employment base that includes the military, tourism, manufacturing, import/export, the university system, and biotech and biomed. Like the Bay Area, it has an enormous number of smart, well-educated people. One-third of the adults have bachelor's degrees or higher.

The heart of the town is military. There are 110,000 uniformed personnel and another 20,000 civilian military personnel (which we can probably double if we include all the contractors to the military). Notably, this is the largest military complement in the industrialized world. And, of course, it can be the largest target.

San Diego County has an enormous number of firms in the world of manufacturing for the military; these produce 75 percent of the world's drones (General Atomics and Northrop Grumman). And there are a dozen more manufacturers of recreational drones (i.e., they don't have bombing capability).

As a result of the exceptional growth and talent at UC San Diego, the county has developed a world-class group of scientists and engineers that have spawned hundreds of major firms and institutes. It is a hotbed of the health-care research industry and, as such, is one of the stars of the venture-capital world.

Tourism (including conventions) stands out as a major employer. A combination of wonderful beaches, the best zoo in the world, SeaWorld (with or without PETA) and Legoland, plus reasonably priced hotels, make San Diego a highly favored resort. It also helps to have twenty-five million people within a day's drive.

Like most of coastal California, this area is patently antibusiness. Doing business in San Diego County is not for the faint of heart. Nonetheless, it is highly attractive to well-educated young professionals and provides a multitude of jobs in a wide range of basic industries.

The county has few social rigidities. There is no social structure or power structure that establishes barriers to entry. For $500, you can be a socialite and get invited to all the wonderful dress-up parties. In places like New York, you go to such dress-up parties to see the grandes dames, the obscenely rich, and the famous. In San Diego, there's nobody to see.

This area is not a bad place to live if you are affluent. Otherwise, it's a bit of a drag, meaning that you may have to commute from Tijuana or Riverside County or one of the tertiary suburbs that require a nasty drive to the employment centers. Public transportation is not one of the highlights of the county. Some of the more populous areas remain totally unserved by transit.

When you see the evening local weather forecast for Southern California, the map inevitably stops at the border as if there were nothing south of it. But I should take a few paragraphs to talk about Tijuana and vicinity.

Tijuana is a bustling town with a multitude of big-name manufacturers in the maquiladora plants. The NAFTA maquiladora "twin plant" concept allows goods to be manufactured, say, in San Diego, then shipped to Tijuana for final assembly with no tax implications. The plants are very highly sophisticated and manufacture pharmaceuticals and other high-dollar goods. The system is a well-oiled machine. An estimated two hundred thousand work in the maquiladora plants in Baja California.

At some point, Baja California will move into second-world status, but it has a long way to go, starting with infrastructure and education and the demise of *mordida* and drug traffic.

An estimated thirty thousand-plus Tijuana citizens cross the border to work in San Diego each day. Without them, San Diego could not function.

Central Valley

Central Valley, also known as the San Joaquin Valley, stretches from Bakersfield up to Stockton. It's not the prettiest place in the world, but it produces an enormous part of our daily diet. Eleven of the top twenty agricultural counties in the state (in terms of dollar production) are in the Central Valley. And half of the nation's fruits, vegetables, and nuts are produced in California.

Central Valley is the food belt of the United States. E&J Gallo, alone, home-based in Modesto, produces 25 percent of all the bottled wine sold in the United States.

The newest crop in the Central Valley is of students. The University of California at Merced is the newest of the UC schools. It opened in 2005 and will celebrate its tenth anniversary this year. When I first visited it in 2005, there was one building. Now there are six thousand students and many buildings. The demographics are 50 percent Hispanic and 27 percent Asian, somewhat different from the mix at most UC schools.

The San Joaquin Valley, because of its strong rail service, is also becoming a popular place to build major warehousing, especially to service Bay Area retailers. To date, Amazon, IKEA, Walmart, and JCPenney have opened distribution centers.

I prefer to think of California in the way that Wallace Stegner does:

> One cannot be pessimistic about the West. This is the native home of hope. When it fully learns that cooperation, not rugged individualism, is the quality that most characterizes and preserves it, then it will have achieved itself and outlived its origins. Then it has a chance to create a society to match its scenery.

Conclusion: California will continue to be a massive economic machine and to add population indefinitely. I see no change in this half-century-long trend. Like making sausage, it may not be pretty, but the results are very tasty and nourishing, even if you don't speak Spanish or an Asian tongue.

Chapter 8: Florida
The Wrinkle State

Way down upon de Swanee Ribber,
Far, far away,
Dere'swha my heart is turning ebber,
Dere'swha de old folks stay.
All up and down de whole creation
Sadly I roam,
Still longing for de old plantation,
And for de old folks at home.

—*Florida State Song*
(before 2008 revisions)

I have been consulting in Florida since the early 1970s and still cannot figure out how the state has survived, economically speaking. It has a population of nineteen million, and I have no idea what it does for a living. It manufactures nothing; it processes nothing; it has no world-class universities; the state's weather is abominable. All it has is Disneyland, but even that gargantuan effort can't support nineteen million people. Florida's really big selling point is that you can get from New York to Miami in three hours (assuming that the plane has no snow delays in New York).

Figure 8.1

What's Good and Bad About Florida	
Good	**Bad**
Cheap housing	Alligators
Cheap everything	Suffocating humidity
Easy to get to from New York	Mosquitoes
Cheap golfing	Swamps
A short hop to Cuba	Hurricanes
	Elderly drivers
	Impossible summers
	No decent jobs

Whereas Con Ed's motto was "Dig we must," Florida's is "Grow we must"—populationwise. I suspect that Florida is a massive Ponzi scheme. If people stop moving there from New York, the entire economy collapses overnight.

A recent AARP study showed that 25 percent of seniors in New York State intend to move to Florida. The IRS-taxpayer migration data shows that in the past decade, more than one million taxpayers moved out of New York. One-third of them moved to Florida. Most brought their bank accounts with them, which is why there is a bank and a stock-brokerage firm on every corner in Florida.

The big march to Florida started after World War II. Prior to that, the state got an initial boost from the start of interstate train service in the early 1900s, when Henry Flagler created a major intrastate line that went all the way down to Key West. (He had a buck or two to spend because he was John D. Rockefeller's partner in Standard Oil.) Florida had actually had intrastate train service before the Civil War, but much of it was destroyed in the war. The auto trains that started in the 1950s and ran from Virginia to Florida actually had had earlier beginnings in the trains running from Florida to New York as early as 1910.

The Great Depression dramatically slowed down Florida's expansion until the late 1930s and then was interrupted again by World War II. In 1963, the railway unions went on strike and caused a massive slowdown of rail travel on the Atlantic seaboard through 1975. Of course, by that time, jet air travel was available to Florida for rather low prices, making passenger-train service somewhat irrelevant. The jet age was a major factor in creating the Gold Coast of Florida with its myriad of hotels and condominiums.

From 1950 to 2013, Florida grew from fewer than three million people to almost twenty million today. Since 1980, the state has grown by more than three hundred thousand residents annually (almost as fast as California).

Figure 8.2

Population Change Florida 1900-2013			
Year	Population	Change from Last Period	Annual Change
1900	528,542	n/a	n/a
1950	2,771,305	2,242,763	44,855
1980	9,746,324	6,975,019	232,501
2013	19,992,000	10,245,676	341,523

Contrary to popular belief, all population growth in Florida is not of seniors. In fact, in the past sixty years, seniors composed only 17 percent of the total population gain. That's a little more than the US average. Of course, within Florida, there are differences in age distribution among the counties.

Figure 8.3

Population by Age Group
State of Florida

% of Population

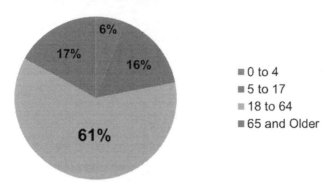

Two-thirds of all of Florida's population gains are in four metropolitan areas: the Gold Coast, Orlando, Tampa/Saint Petersburg, and Jacksonville. The other thirty-four counties share one-third of the population gains.

The dominating growth has been in the Gold Coast, which includes three counties: Dade (Miami), Broward (Fort Lauderdale), and Palm Beach. In the past thirty years, those three counties have added almost 2.5 million persons. Orlando is in second place, with Tampa/Saint Petersburg and Jacksonville lagging behind. The latter three areas don't have much attraction for New Yorkers, so their growth has been slower.

Notably, the state's population has doubled in the past thirty years. That's impressive.

Figure 8.4

Population by Metropolitan Area State of Florida 1980-2010				
Metropolitan Area	1980	2010	Change	%
Gold Coast				
Dade (Miami)	1,625,781	2,496,457	870,676	54%
Broward (Ft. Lauderdale)	1,018,200	1,748,066	729,866	72%
Palm Beach	576,863	1,320,134	743,271	129%
Total Gold Coast	**3,220,844**	**5,564,657**	**2,343,813**	**73%**
Orlando	804,925	2,134,406	1,329,481	165%
Tampa/St. Petersburg	1,613,603	2,783,427	1,169,824	72%
Jacksonville	737,541	1,345,596	608,055	82%
Total 4 Major Metros	**6,376,913**	**11,828,086**	**5,451,173**	**85%**
Other 34 Counties	**3,369,411**	**6,973,246**	**3,603,835**	**107%**
Total Florida	**9,746,324**	**18,801,332**	**9,055,008**	**93%**

The rate of population gain is anticipated to slow down a bit in the 2010–2040 period, but the state is still anticipated to gain another 6.8 million people in that thirty-year time span.

Figure 8.5

Population Projections Major Metropolitan Areas State of Florida 2010-2040				
Area	2010	2040	Change	% Change
Florida	18,801,332	25,603,577	6,802,245	36%
Gold Coast	5,564,657	7,005,514	1,440,857	26%
Orlando	2,134,406	3,394,228	1,259,822	59%
Tampa/St. Petersburg	2,783,427	3,771,458	988,031	35%
Jacksonville	1,345,596	1,876,463	530,867	39%

Source: Univ. of Florida, Bureau of Economic and Business Research

On a percentage basis, Orlando takes the lead at 59 percent growth, but in the pure population count, the Gold Coast continues to lead the pack with a projected 1.4 million gain in the 2010–2040 period.

In terms of ethnicity, in 1980, the state was 9 percent Hispanic. By 2010, that percentage had increased to 22. The black population, as a percentage of the total, remained relatively stable. The non-Hispanic white population declined from 77 percent of the total change to 62 percent in that time frame. (In old census data for Florida, it is notable that, until 1860, the black population there was divided into free blacks and slave blacks.)

Figure 8.6

Ethnicity by Percent State of Florida 1980-2010			
Census year	Black	Hispanic origin (of any race)	White, not of Hispanic origin
1980	14%	9%	77%
2010	16%	22%	62%

Florida population gains can be segmented into natural increase (births over deaths), domestic migration, and international migration. The natural increase has been fairly steady. The big change is in the proportion of the population gain that is international.

Figure 8.7

Components of Population Change in Percent State of Florida 1980-2013			
Category	1980-1990	1990-2000	2010-2013
Natural Increase	13%	15%	16%
Domestic Increase	n/a	64%	42%
International Increase	n/a	30%	42%
Total	13%	109%	100%

And remember, this is long after the Cuban immigration. The new international immigration tends to be both European and Brazilian. São Paulo is an eight-hour flight directly north to Miami. And Europe is just a five-hour hop.

When the boom was burgeoning, there were planeloads of Europeans being brought to Florida by entities that would sell them new-subdivision homes. Dozens of European magazines hyped the Florida experience. In raw numbers, the 1980s saw the first superwave of great domestic migration, with over two million Americans moving to Florida in the 1980s and also in the 1990s.

Figure 8.8

			Components of Change State of Florida 1980-2013				
Timeframe	Total Pop. Increase	Natural Increase (Births - Deaths)	Birth	Deaths	Net Migration (Domestic + Int'l)	Source of Migration	
					Total	Intl	Domestic
2010-2013	740,049	121,075	697,507	576,432	618,974	310,822	308,152
1990-2000	3,044,307	448,216	1,931,148	1,482,932	2,596,091	649,023	1,947,068
1980-1990	3,190,965	420,867	1,614,057	1,193,190	2,770,098	n/a	n/a

The age profile varies significantly by metropolitan area. Tampa/Saint Petersburg is the leader in the sixty-five-and-older category, with 17.3 percent of its population in that age group, with the Gold Coast slightly behind it.

Figure 8.9

	Age Distribution Major Metropolitan Areas State of Florida 2010			
	Percent distribution			
Metropolitan Area	Under 18 years	18 to 44 years	45 to 64 years	65+
Gold Coast	21.7	36.0	26.4	16.0
Orlando	23.4	38.9	25.4	12.4
Tampa/St. Petersburg	21.2	33.9	27.7	17.3
Jacksonville	23.8	36.7	27.4	12.1
Florida	21.3	34.4	27.0	17.3

Orlando and Jacksonville have age profiles much like normal communities elsewhere in the Sunbelt, with only 12 percent of the population over age sixty-five.

Cost of Living

One of the key factors that has drawn folks from the Northeast to Florida is the cost of living. Just about everything appears to be cheaper in Florida. Not that I would ever consider living there, but compared the cost of living in Miami to that of San Diego, my longtime home base.

The most obvious differential is in the cost of housing, but Florida is also a lot cheaper in almost every other category, too. The consumer-cost index actually overstates the cost of living in Florida because it does not include the giveaways that are always available, particularly in supermarkets. I haven't figured out how they do it, but the stores continually have an abundance of two-for-one sales.

As I go around the United States, I generally find that prices relate to household income. Places that have low household incomes, like Florida, have lower prices than places with higher incomes. Some of that has to do with the cost of labor, but most of it has to do with affordability. If you can pay more, retailers will charge more.

Figure 8.10

Cost of Living Comparison Miami and San Diego 2014			
Index	Miami, FL	San Diego, CA	% Difference
Overall index	104	126	20.50%
Groceries	108	106	-1.40%
Housing	100	170	69.40%
Utilities	94	113	20.70%
Transportation	107	107	0.40%
Healthcare	111	112	0.50%
Goods & Services	108	104	-3.80%

Source: Council for Community and Economic Research

The most poignant evidence of the differential between Florida and San Diego is the cost of housing and utilities. For reasons unknown, home insurance costs 76 percent more in San Diego than in Miami. Florida predictably has hurricanes. In San Diego, the last earthquake was ten thousand years ago. I don't get it. And Miamians need heat and air conditioning year-round; San Diego doesn't—yet their electric bills are one-third lower.

Figure 8.11

Cost of Housing and Utilities Miami and San Diego 2014			
Item	Miami, FL	San Diego, CA	San Diego, CA
Apt Rent	$1,279.67	$1,772.40	38.50%
Home Insurance	$1,133.00	$1,997.04	76.30%
Electrical Bill	$101.27	$136.98	35.30%
Total Energy	$150.69	$189.75	25.90%

Source: Council for Community and Economic Research

The Employment Base

Florida lost eight hundred thousand jobs in the recent recession. In 2007, it peaked out at more than 8 million jobs but by 2010 had dipped to 7.2 million. One-third of the total job losses were in the construction trades. If you add in the building-related industries like finance and sales at outlets like Home Depot, almost half of the jobs lost in Florida were construction related.

Losses in the three key Florida industries (leisure/hospitality, education, and health services) were negligible. Almost one-third of all payroll jobs in Florida are in those three industries, so basically, the recession in Florida was construction based. True, it lost some manufacturing jobs, but manufacturing accounts for only 4 percent of all payroll jobs.

Unemployment peaked at 11 percent in 2008 and has now settled down to a palatable 6 percent, even though the construction industry has barely rebounded.

As long as folks keep coming to Florida, its payrolls will continue to expand. And as soon as its construction industry blossoms again (and it will), Florida will see its entire economy resuscitated.

Figure 8.12

	Total	Construction	Mfg	Leisure & Hospitality	Education & Health Services
Payroll Employment, Selected Industries (000)					
State of Florida					
June 2004 - June 2014					
2004	7,476	569	411	925	938
2005	7,752	633	415	952	957
2006	7,990	692	418	963	985
2007	8,027	634	401	984	1,018
2008	7,743	522	373	975	1,038
2009	7,221	398	323	926	1,048
2010	7,185	354	309	931	1,071
2011	7,232	332	312	954	1,089
2012	7,390	340	317	997	1,110
2013	7,563	363	321	1,036	1,124
2014	7,798	403	327	1,077	1,158

Source: Bureau of Labor Statistics

The Four Big Metros

The Gold Coast

I am tempted to say that the Gold Coast is tarnished, but that just isn't true. It continues to be an enormous draw to foreign civilians like Brazilians, Europeans, and New Yorkers.

Between the Gold Coast counties, there are major differences in demographics. For instance, 65 percent of the population in Dade County is Hispanic, compared to only 25 percent in Broward and 19 percent in Palm Beach County. Palm Beach County has the highest median age of the three, yet its percentage of population over sixty-five is much lower than in Dade County. In terms of household size, the average is highest in Dade County, followed by Broward and Palm Beach Counties.

Figure 8.13

Demographic Statistics Gold Coast Counties 2010			
Category	Dade	Broward	Palm Beach
Median Age	38	39.7	43.5
% over 65	21.6%	14.1%	14.3%
% Hispanic	65.0%	25.1%	19.0%
Avg. Household Size	2.83	2.52	2.39

Statistically speaking, the Gold Coast counties get richer and more educated as you go north. Thus, in Palm Beach County 33 percent of the population has a bachelors' degree or higher compared to Dade County's 26 percent.

The same situation is true for median household income and the percentage of households with incomes over $100,000.

Also, home ownership increases substantially as you go northward. In Dade County, 54 percent own a home compared to 72 percent in Palm Beach County, and in Palm Beach County, 36 percent of owned homes have no mortgages compared to 33 percent in Dade County.

I also looked at the great state of California and the nation to see how Florida compares to each of them. The most poignant differential is that in California, only 21 percent of homeowners have no mortgage compared to 35 percent in Florida, but you could have guessed that anyhow. Also, in California, 27 percent of households have incomes over $100,000 compared to 18 percent in Florida. The higher cost of living in California relates to household incomes which are higher in California. It all evens out in the end.

Figure 8.14

Evidence of Affluence Gold Coast Counties						
Category	Dade	Broward	Palm Beach	Florida	California	U.S.
Bachelor's Degree or Higher	26%	30%	33%	26%	31%	29%
Median Household Income	$ 43,464	$ 51,603	$ 52,806	$ 47,309	$ 61,400	$ 53,046
% of Households with more than $100,000 Income	17%	22%	23%	18%	27%	20%
% of Homeowners without a Mortgage	33%	26%	36%	35%	21%	36%
Own their home	54%	67%	72%	68%	56%	66%

Orlando

Orlando is the world's playground. It gets more tourists than any city in the United States (and maybe the world). In 2013, Orlando played host to a record fifty-seven million, whose out-of-control spending generated $7 billion in tax revenues. One of every three jobs in Orlando is tourism related. Orlando has 450 hotels/motels and 118,000 rooms (second only to Las Vegas).

Figure 8.15

Main Tourist Attractions Orlando	
Big Time	Side Shows (Partial List)
Disney	Chocolate Kingdom
Magic Kingsdom	Scream' Gator Zip Line
Epcot	Dinosaur World
Animal Kingdom	Gator Land
Hollywood Studio	Discovery Cove
	Madame Taussaud
Universal Studios	WetnWild
Legoland	Ripley's Believe It or Not
Sea World	Capone's Dinner & Show

The only Disney attraction that leaves me cold is Hollywood Studios. It's as boring as the California original.

Tampa/Saint Petersburg

I have visited the Tampa/Saint Petersburg area numerous times over the years and cannot figure out what drives the economy there. It is highly possible that assisted living, memory care, and other health services are the base of the local economy. The statistics show that one out of every four jobs is in health services, but I think it is higher than that.

I don't have much else to say about the Tampa/Saint Petersburg area except that it has nice beaches, but then again, so does the rest of Florida.

Jacksonville

Jacksonville: now, there's a normal city. It is the gateway to Florida, just across the state line from Georgia. It has a normal complement of population and a normal distribution of jobs.

It is a water-related town with the largest deepwater port in the South and is the largest auto importer on the East Coast. It is the largest transportation and distribution center in the state. It is also a military town, with thirty thousand uniformed personnel and twenty thousand civilians attached to the military.

It is named after General Andrew Jackson (who, incidentally, never visited the city). And its primary claim to fame is that it has the largest urban park system in the United States, with 111,000 acres of parks (so sayeth the Chamber of Commerce).

It is not your typical Florida tourism town but a nice place to work and live.

Conclusion: If living in a year-round, screened-in environment is your thing, Florida is definitely the place for you. Ditto if you like to live really cheaply. Little by little, Florida is turning into an enclave for Europeans, Brazilians, and "New Yawkers," and those three immigrant groups will keep Florida growing indefinitely.

One last thought: Florida is also a great place to buy used Cadillacs in great condition as the aging population inevitably and reluctantly tosses its car keys to CarMax.

Chapter 9: Metropolitan Areas
The Winners and the Losers

Cities have always been the fireplaces of civilization, whence light and heat radiated out into the dark, cold world.

—Theodore Parker

Most of us live in metropolitan areas. That's just the way it is nowadays. Some of us have the good fortune to live in metropolitan areas that are on the cusp of greatness; others live in metros that are either survivors or suffering the pains of ultimate stagnation.

In this chapter, I examine some two dozen metropolitan areas, segmenting them into fast-growing, survivor, and stagnant categories.

The **fast-growing** metropolitan areas typically hug the West Coast; they are also found in the Southeast, a couple of Mountain states, and the self-proclaimed Great State of Texas.

The **survivors** are typically in states that have very strong bases in finance, world-renowned educational and/or health-care institutions, and/or have highly stable modern manufacturing. In addition, they have stable populations. They also tend to have very strong and perpetually well-funded cultural bases.

The **stagnant** metropolitan areas are those that have nongrowing or shrinking populations; their populations are also aging rapidly, depleting the workforce. The stagnant metropolitan areas also have stagnant employment bases and may have governmental pension-fund obligations in their central cities that are on the verge of bankruptcy and unable to carry on typical municipal functions.

The metropolitan areas I survey in this book are listed here. There are many more that would fit in each category, but I had to limit the number just for practicality's sake. I have visited every one of the metropolitan areas I mention in the book, except for Dayton, Ohio. I'll get there one day. I understand it has a great air museum.

Figure 9.1

Analyzed Metropolitan Areas United States		
Fast Growing	**Surviving 12**	**Stagnant**
Atlanta	Baltimore	Buffalo
Austin	Boston	Cleveland
Dallas	Chicago	Dayton
Denver	Cincinnati	Detroit
San Diego	Columbus	Milwaukee
San Francisco	Indianapolis	Pittsburgh, PA
San Jose	Kansas City	Rochester
Seattle	Minneapolis-St. Paul	
	New York	
	Oklahoma City	
	Philadelphia	
	St. Louis	

The Economic Formula Indicating the Success or Failure of Metropolitan Areas

Somewhere along the line, I have mentioned that two-thirds of our gross domestic product is consumer spending. Now I want to dig a little deeper into that subject, because it is paramount to the success or failure of states and metropolitan areas.

For every state and metropolitan area, a very rigid formula defines its economy. Every time one basic job is added, two support jobs are created. One of the support jobs services the basic job and the other one services the consumer.

The key here is the **basic job**. A basic job is defined as one whose source of revenue is from outside its own metropolitan area. Thus, for example, San Diego has multiple basic job sources: military, tourism, manufacturing, and import/export, among others. Virtually all the funding for those industries is imported; for example, the military's is from Washington, and tourism is funded by folks who have earned their money somewhere else.

The 1:2 ratio of job types is of vital importance. If a metropolitan area does not have a growing basic-job machine, its economy falters. And, as the economy falters, folks with marketable job skills leave the area, and eventually, mainly people who need and use extensive governmental services remain.

When the basic jobs leave, the support jobs have a smaller pool of customers to support them and their revenues decline and employment declines.

Pointedly, when the basic jobs falter, local government revenue declines as the sources of income (the failing basic industry and the well-paying jobs) contract. And then, the metropolitan area goes into bankruptcy. Or, more specifically, the key city in the metropolitan area does, while the suburban communities just muddle through. Meanwhile, the bankrupt city looks to Washington for support, and that just isn't available anymore. So the Detroits and Buffalos of the world slowly fail. It is inevitable.

The Aging of the Metros

The median age in the fast-growing metros is distinctly lower than in the less fortunate ones. In the fast-growing metros, the median age is 35.4 years; in the survivors, it is 36.7 years, and in the stagnant metros, 39.8 years.

Figure 9.2

Median Age in Metro Region Types
Continental United States
2010

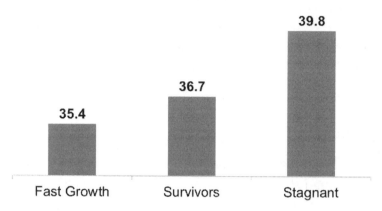

		39.8
	36.7	
35.4		
Fast Growth	Survivors	Stagnant

In the sixty-five-and-over category, the fast-growing metros account for only 10.5 percent of the population; the survivor metros for 11.9 percent, and the stagnant metros, 14.6 percent.

Figure 9.3

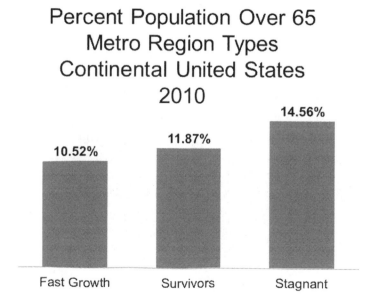

Percent Population Over 65
Metro Region Types
Continental United States
2010

		14.56%
	11.87%	
10.52%		
Fast Growth	Survivors	Stagnant

In keeping with the prior discussion on why metros grow, the following table compares the population changes in the metropolitan areas. Those in the four fast-growing regions (Texas, Southeast, West Coast, and Mountain) tended to triple in size from 1950 to 2010. Conversely, the survivors and stagnant metropolitan areas (predominant)

Figure 9.4

Population Change by Percent Metropolitan Areas, by Region 1980-2010		
Region	1950-2010	1980-2010
Texas	395.7%	106.8%
Southeast	382.0%	90.2%
West Coast	286.7%	69.9%
Mountain	291.8%	52.6%
Midwest	95.5%	23.5%
Northeast	15.7%	12.7%
Total	287%	54.0%

Here are the numbers behind the percentages:

Figure 9.5

	Population Change Selected Metropolitan Areas, by Region 1950-1980-2010		
	Population Change		
Region	**1950-2010**	**1950-1980**	**1980-2010**
Metropolitan Area Total	**110,188,292**	**46,479,941**	**63,708,351**
Texas	**13,575,500**	4,793,756	8,781,744
Southeast	**41,054,410**	14,654,440	26,399,970
West Coast	**31,873,592**	14,186,882	17,686,710
Mountain	**2,731,640**	1,467,693	1,263,947
Total	**89,235,142**	**35,102,771**	**54,132,371**
Midwest	**12,870,535**	6,642,097	6,228,438
Northeast	**8,082,615**	4,735,073	3,347,542
Total	**20,953,150**	**11,377,170**	**9,575,980**
Texas/Southeast/West Coast/Mountain as % of Total	**81.0%**	**75.5%**	**85.0%**

Even as we look at the past thirty years, we can see the strong growth in the four fast-growing regions and the relatively minute growth in the Midwest and Northeast.

We can also look at the recovery pattern in the past three years in terms of employment. The categories I examined were total payroll jobs, manufacturing, information industries, and financial services. Compare the fast-growing metropolitan areas with those that are survivors or stagnant. The high-growth areas had consistent growth in the four job categories, while the other metro areas just sort of muddled through.

The one anomaly is the manufacturing sector in the stagnant metropolitan areas. Its higher percentages result from modest returns to life after dramatic recessionary downturns rather than any boom in its industries.

Figure 9.6

Comparison of Employment Growth Selected Industries High Growth, Low Growth and Stagnant Metropolitan Areas 2011-2013			
	% Employment Change		
Type of Industry	High Growth	Low Growth	Stagnant
Total Payroll Jobs	7.2%	3.1%	2.3%
Manufacturing	2.2%	0.3%	4.1%
Information	5.3%	0.9%	-1.0%
Financial Services	6.7%	3.0%	0.6%

The Future of the Metros

The population-projection patterns established in past decades should repeat themselves in the future. As we look out to 2040 for the metropolitan areas examined here, it is notable that the fast-growing ones are projected to gain 54 percent, and the survivors, 12 percent. The stagnant ones will lose 2 percent of their current population.

From a pure numbers standpoint, the fast-growing metropolitan areas are projected to gain more than 15.9 million people in the 2010–2040 time frame while the survivors add 4.6 million and the stagnant metros lose a couple of hundred thousand.

Figure 9.7

Population Projection Selected Metropolitan Areas 2010-2040				
			Change 2010-2040	
Category	2010	2040	No.	%
Fast Growing	29,630,000	45,554,000	15,924,000	54%
Survivors	29,731,263	34,361,000	4,629,737	16%
Stagnant	13,317,398	13,102,000	(215,398)	-2%

Like the states they are in, the fast-growing metropolitan areas derive a substantial percentage of population growth from immigration, while the survivors and stagnant metropolitan areas rely almost entirely on natural change for their population gains, if they have any at all.

In the stagnant category, the natural change is wildly over 100 percent because, statistically, many of them have emigration.

Figure 9.8

Natural and Inmigration Population Change Fast Growing, Survivor and Stagnant Metropolitan Area 2010-2013		
% of each Category	Natural Change	Change from Inmigration
Fast Growing	50.2%	113.5%
Survivors	79.2%	18.9%
Stagnant	212.6%	-9.4%

Immigration has two components: domestic and international. The table below shows that in the fast-growing metropolitan areas, two-thirds of the migration is international, while in the surviving metros, the reverse is true. And in the stagnant metros, the number of domestic immigrants is meager, and the international migration is negative.

Figure 9.9

Source of Migration Fast Growing, Survivor and Stagnant Metropolitan Areas 2010-2013		
Category	International	Domestic
Fast Growing	661,615	315,330
Survivors	268,893	772,961
Stagnant	(33,240)	68,419

Fast Growing Metropolitan Areas

The fast-growing metropolitan areas follow the patterns of fast-growing states. Perhaps the overriding factor in all of these metropolitan areas is an enormous number of very bright young professionals who, in essence, have created the industries that form the basis for the success of these metropolitan areas.

Uniformly, the areas have renowned research universities, innumerable start-ups in technology (particularly in software and health services), an exceptional social scene and, for the most part, decent climates. Their great successes did not happen overnight. Most have been in the development stage for thirty or forty years, a period that coincides with the maturation of the computer, electronics, venture-capitalism, and health-care industries, and, of course, the inevitable web. Most of them have great water bodies or mountains nearby, with skiing within a few hours' drive.

There are many other areas that fit this fast-growing category, but there's only so much room in this book. I don't want to insult the folks in Raleigh-Durham, Washington, DC, Orange County, or Los Angeles, for they, too, fit in this fast-growing category. (I inevitably leave out Houston in my writing because, although it is fast growing and has wonderful medical services, it has such a horrible climate and impossible traffic patterns, coupled with choking air from the oil and gas industries, that it pains me to include it.)

Figure 9.10

Reasons for Fast Growth Selected High Growth Metropolitan Areas	
Metropolitan Area	Reason for Fast Growth
San Diego	Great climate; great brains
San Francisco	OK climate; great brains
San Jose	OK climate; great brains
Denver	Great skiing; young educated workforce
Dallas	Amazing job machine
Austin	UT Austin & strong job machine
Seattle	Wet with great jobs for techies
Atlanta	Mecca

The Surviving Dozen

There are a dozen metropolitan areas that I categorize as survivors. Despite low rates of population growth and most often dismal climates, they have so much going for them in terms of great universities, vibrant lifestyles, strong employment bases, and exceptionally strong art and culture and vibrant center cities that they will continue to prosper.

Most often, they once relied heavily on manufacturing for their strength but have managed to create new industries that have allowed them to maintain solvent economies. By and large, manufacturing has faded somewhat, but the financial industries, headquarters of operations, and high-tech and health-care services have allowed them to attract a highly educated workforce.

It is inevitable that the Northeast metros like Boston, New York, and Philadelphia will continue to prosper, much of the reason being their proximity to Europe. After all, from the Northeast metros, it is the same air time to London as it is to Los Angeles. In fact, Boston, New York, and Philadelphia all have very European airs about them in their central cores.

The Midwest has numerous metropolitan areas that have proven themselves capable of surviving, although many of the smaller towns throughout the Midwest are languishing.

A major part of the success of the surviving dozen is that they almost all have cultures of philanthropy that have allowed them to have great museums and great music and culture. These metros inevitably have numerous exceptionally wealthy and generous individuals and companies that open their checkbooks and have been contributing to their communities for a century or more.

In most of the surviving dozen, there is an old-boy component that can make things happen, including the building of great sport venues and great teams. Historically, it has also created great newspapers.

Figure 9.11

Reasons for Survival Surviving Dozen Metropolitan Areas		
Metropolitan Area	**State**	**Reasons for Survival**
Baltimore	Maryland	Proximity to D.C.
Boston	Massachusetts	Brain Center of the NE
Chicago	Illinois	Strong Financial Center
Cincinnati	Ohio	Major Basic Employers
Columbus	Ohio	Strong Basic Employers
Indianapolis	Indiana	Strong Pharmaceutical Base
Kansas City	Kansas	Solid Basic Industries
Minneapolis/St. Paul	Minnesota	Strong Basic Employers
New York	New York	Center of the World
Oklahoma City	Oklahoma	Oil/Health Care
Philadelphia	Pennsylvania	Proximity to NY
St. Louis	Missouri	Strong Basic Employers

The big daddy of Midwest success is Chicago, which is not only a bustling town but has manufactured an amazing central city, second only to New York in the United States. It has a remarkable selection of eateries, music and cultural venues, and an exceptional selection of housing in its central core—and a great transportation system. And, thanks to a highly dynamic series of heavyweight mayors and their minions, Chicago has remained a dynamo. You can't be a wimpy mayor in Chicago.

A similar picture can be painted on a smaller scale for the other surviving metropolitan areas. When you visit these metros, you can smell success.

What is particularly of interest to me is how the Midwest survivors have worked very hard to create a vibrant downtown where often, there was once almost none. In the past two decades, cities like Cincinnati, Baltimore, and Minneapolis have invested heavily in their midtowns and have drawn new employers and the yuppie component into their cores.

They have worked hard to bring new industry into the midtowns, particularly start-ups that attract the young, college-educated crowd. It is this crowd that allows the eateries and bars and upscale clothing venues to prosper in an urban setting.

It can also be mentioned that the demographic changes discussed earlier in the book have powerful effects on the midtown expansions. The combination of later marriages and later children mean dual-income households and with lots of disposable funds. I should mention that this yuppie crowd has also been a boon to the travel industry, the upscale-automobile industry, and sports attendance and is the mainstay of such purveyors as Nordstrom and Best Buy. It likes new things.

Let me focus now on two midsize Midwest metropolitan areas that are surviving nicely: Minneapolis and Indianapolis.

Minneapolis/Saint Paul

Minneapolis/Saint Paul is the second-largest economic center in the Midwest behind Chicago.

Both Saint Paul and Minneapolis lost thousands of manufacturing jobs in the recent downturn, and neither has recovered them. But growth has returned in professional work and to the Twin Cities-area hub of banking, finance, law, accounting, advertising, and public relations.

Business and professional services employment had a small setback in 2009–2010 but has moved forward steadily since then.

Figure 9.12

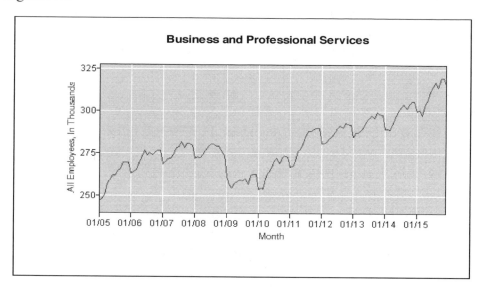

During the recession, the Minneapolis unemployment rate barely topped 8 percent, well below the national average, and now has an unemployment rate below 4 percent—among the five lowest rates in the country.

Figure 9.13

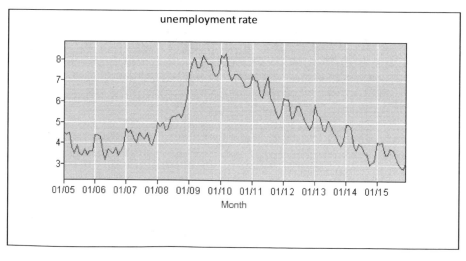

The Twin Cities is home to more corporate headquarters per capita than anywhere in the nation. Included here are Target, U.S. Bancorp, Ameriprise Financial, and Excel Energy.

The Twin Cities also has an extremely well-funded cultural scene, thanks to a century of support by major manufacturers. The Minneapolis Foundation administers over nine hundred charitable funds. Of equal interest is that fact that more than 40 percent of adults give time to volunteer work, the highest percentage of any metropolitan area in the nation.

Drawback: It's a bit...chilly...in the winter.

Indianapolis

Indianapolis suffered a major employment decline in 2009–2010, like much of the Midwest, but has bounced back nicely.

Figure 9.14

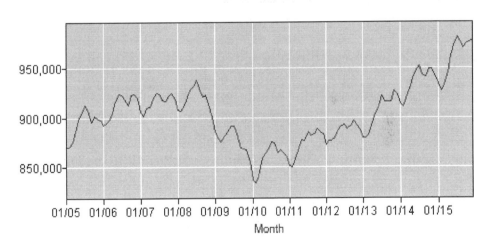

Biotechnology, life sciences, and health care are major sectors of the economy, bolstered by the headquarters presences of Eli Lilly, Roche Diagnostics, and Dow Agro-Sciences.

It is also a major distribution center, with fifteen hundred distribution firms that employ more than a hundred thousand workers. It is home to the second-largest FedEx hub in the world. Like most distribution centers, it is ringed by such distributors as Amazon, Coca-Cola, CVS Caremark, and O'Reilly Auto Parts.

As a result of its diverse economy, its unemployment rate, which peaked at 10 percent, has moved smartly downward and is now at the 4 percent level.

Figure 9.15

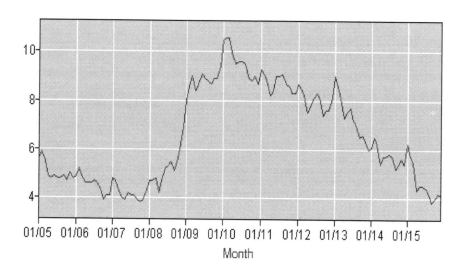

Indianapolis is a major sports and tourism center, thanks to the Indy 500 and the largest half marathon in the United States, and it labels itself as the "amateur sports capital of the world." It is the headquarters of the National Collegiate Athletic Association and the National Federation of State High School Associations.

The Stagnant

Here are seven metropolitan areas that are just plain stagnant. Their major problem is that their employment base has not kept up with the times. They are former manufacturing dynamos that have lost their way.

The seven are, in alphabetical order, Buffalo, Cleveland, Dayton, Detroit, Milwaukee, Pittsburgh, and Rochester.

Figure 9.16

Reasons for Demise Stagnant Metropolitan Areas	
Metropolitan Area	**Reason For Survival**
Buffalo	Declining Base Industries & Stagnant Pop.
Cleveland-Elyria, OHCleveland	Declining Base Industries & Stagnant Pop.
Dayton	Declining Base Industries & Stagnant Pop.
Detroit	Declining Base Industries & Stagnant Pop.
Milwaukee	Declining Base Industries & Stagnant or Declining Pop.
Pittsburgh	Declining Base Industries & Stagnant Pop.
Rochester	Declining Base Industries & Stagnant Pop.

Much has been made of the revival of Detroit. Unfortunately, there is far more talk than revival. Yes, GM and Ford and Chrysler still have a few plants in Michigan, but other states have eaten Detroit's cake, as I pointed out in the chapter on manufacturing. The Detroit metro inevitably has a demographic problem as well, with its workforce growing older and a growing shortage of employment-ready youth.

Today's automobile industry does not relate to yesterday's world. The automobile plants of yesterday required strong backs and the willingness to do repetitive tasks for years on end. Not so today. The plants today are engineering marvels that require employees to understand math and to be able to read and understand complicated robotic dynamics. Unfortunately, Detroit is not spawning that type of employee.

The center city of Detroit remains a disaster. Dozens of major, once-glorious structures remain empty, awaiting a revival that will be long in coming. The money in Detroit continues to hide out in Grosse Pointe, Auburn, and Bloomfield Hills.

The only really good thing about Detroit is that the housing is insanely cheap. The median price of a home in the City of Detroit is less than $50,000, and sales activity is dismal.

The finest home in Detroit recently sold. It was the Fisher Mansion (for the family of Fisher Body fame). It is in the very best neighborhood of Detroit, has fifteen thousand square feet, fifteen bedrooms and seventeen bathrooms, and sits on two acres. It sold for $1.6 million, which is slightly over $100 per square foot.

Note that a home of that type in west Los Angeles would most likely sell for close to $1,000 per square foot, and there would be active bidding for it. And oh, yes, it is next door to the home where Mitt Romney grew up.

Conclusion: Like music, food and drink, and clothing, preferences change over time. In today's America, the preference is clearly the ability to live in a hospitable climate near water and mountains and to utilize one's education and skills in many of the industries that have been created in the past quarter century.

Chapter 10: A House is Not a Home: It is an Annuity

Every person who invests in <u>well-selected</u> real estate...adopts the surest and safest method of becoming independent, for real estate is the basis of wealth.

—Theodore Roosevelt

©Justin Cox

In this chapter, I address the issue of housing supply and demand, the quality of US housing stock, and trends in tenure (ownership vs. renting).

First, it is important to recognize the remarkable progress we have made in technology since the end of World War II as it applies to our housing stock. In 1950, a substantial number of our states did not have indoor plumbing, and many didn't have phones available in their homes. Thirty years later, virtually everybody had indoor plumbing and telephone service. And now, almost everyone has a cellular phone. So we have been doing something right.

The major progress has been made in the Southern states, which had almost no indoor plumbing in 1950 (sayeth the census), and half the folks there didn't have telephones in 1960. The North virtually all had indoor plumbing in 1950 (a climate-induced facility), and almost everyone had a telephone.

Figure 10.1

Plumbing and Telephones Selected States 1950-2010				
	Incomplete Plumbing		No Telephone Available	
State	1950	1980	1960	1980
Low-Flush				
Alabama	68%	5%	41%	13%
Arkansas	71%	5%	49%	13%
Kentucky	64%	8%	39%	11%
Mississippi	74%	7%	55%	17%
South Carolina	65%	5%	45%	13%
Full House				
California	17%	1%	17%	5%
Washington D.C.	11%	2%	17%	5%
Massachusetts	19%	2%	13%	4%
New Jersey	15%	2%	15%	5%
Utah	18%	1%	13%	5%

Our **housing stock** is getting old and needs to be replenished and renewed. The median age of an owner-occupied home is thirty-eight years and a renter-occupied unit, forty-two years. Almost one in five owner-occupied housing units and one in four renter-occupied units were built prior to 1950. Obviously, this doesn't compare to the average age of homes in Europe, but those homes were made to last. Ours really weren't, especially in the South and West.

Figure 10.2

Age of the Housing Stock United States				
Year Built	Owner Occupied		Renter Occupied	
	No.	%	No.	%
Prior to 1950	13,934	18%	9,614	25%
1950-1980	30,133	40%	16,708	43%
1980-2010	32,026	42%	12,494	32%
Total	76,093	100%	38,816	100%
Median Age	38		42	

Across the nation, about two-thirds of all households own their own homes. In the Midwest, it is often as high as 75 percent ownership, and in others, like California, it is 55 percent. Each state, through time, arrives at its own equilibrium level of own-to-rent ratio.

The US average of home ownership was 64 percent in the 1980 census and the same in 2010. California—a state that forever bemoans its unaffordability of housing—had 55 percent ownership in 1980 and the same in 2010. Nothing has changed.

Figure 10.3

Home Ownership Rates Selected States 1980 and 2010		
State	1980	2010
United States	64.0%	64.0%
California	55.0%	55.0%
Florida	68.0%	67.0%
Texas	64.0%	63.0%
Colorado	65.0%	65.0%
Minnesota	72.0%	73.0%
Iowa	72.0%	72.0%

When politicos try to change the home-ownership ratios, it can be disastrous. Thus, the Bush push to increase home ownership in the early to mid-2000s through the loosening of lending criteria, proved disastrous for those states that pursued it with a vengeance (like California, Arizona, Nevada, and Florida). Currently, the national housing market is back in equilibrium and, I suspect, will remain that way for the foreseeable future. And that's good.

Owner-occupied housing is a good thing. Ownership provides **stability for a household**. It is also a savings account as a result of mortgage amortization. If you live in the house long enough, you will pay off the mortgage. The term *mortgage* is based on the French word for death—*mort*—thus, over time, you can kill your mortgage. Kill it with kindness. But, as we learned in the more recent recession, a mortgage can also be deadly.

A mortgage is also one of the only dependable **tax shelters** for most households. You can deduct the interest you pay on the mortgage. The United States is one of few countries that allows such a deduction. Canada did away with it decades ago.

It is also a **safety net** if emergency needs surface. Assuming you have some equity in the home, you can borrow against it. I obviously do not condone borrowing against your home to buy boats, luxury cars, or go on round-the-world cruises. That is stealing from your piggy bank.

But what I particularly like about eventually owning a house free and clear is that it can provide you with a **guaranteed annuity** when you retire. Through the vehicle of the **reverse mortgage**, you can create tax-free income that is federally insured.

Say your house is worth $400,000 and you are sixty-two years old (the minimum qualifying age for a reverse mortgage). If you get your reverse mortgage during a period of low interest rates, you could qualify to receive guaranteed payments of $1,112 every month for as long as you keep your home as your primary residence. (If interest rates are higher when you get your reverse mortgage, the amount you qualify for will be lower.)

According to Bruce McPherson, a certified reverse-mortgage specialist, the payments you receive are tax-free because they are technically loan proceeds. But the big difference between a reverse mortgage and other mortgages is that you are never required to service the loan. In other words, all interest is deferred until you have died or permanently vacated your home. Until that day arrives, the tax-free payments you receive are guaranteed to continue—even if you live an incredibly long time, and even if home values fall.

Someday, when your children inherit your home, they can choose to sell it and keep the net proceeds (just like when a home is sold with any type of mortgage on it). Or, your family can choose to keep the home by paying back the loan balance. If the home is underwater, your family will be glad to know that the reverse mortgage loan balance is **never** a personal liability; it is only attached to the home. They can walk away, or they can choose to keep the home by paying just 95 percent of the appraised value instead of the entire loan balance!

I can't think of a better investment than that.

With that lecture completed, let me discuss the nation's housing market and where it is heading. In this chapter, I will discuss owned homes, condominiums, and apartments.

There are, in this nation, approximately 115 million occupied housing units. Structurally speaking, this mass of housing is segmented into 73,762,000 single-family homes, 8,059,000 condominiums and cooperatives, 26,204,000 apartments, and 7,190,000 mobile homes, according to the 2011 Census Bureau's American Housing Survey.

Looking a little deeper into the numbers, we learn that of the owner-occupied housing, more than 85 percent is single-family detached housing. Condominiums and cooperatives share the balance with mobile homes. Condominiums and cooperatives are typically highly urban products, while mobile homes are located mostly in the nonurban areas, particularly in the Southeast.

For renters, almost two-thirds are in traditional apartments, but more than a quarter are renting single-family homes.

Figure 10.4

Housing Types, by Tenure (000's) United States						
	Owner Occupied		Renter Occupied		Total	
Category	No.	%	No.	%	No.	%
Single Family Detached Homes	62,662	85.5%	11,099	26.5%	73,762	64.0%
Condominium/Cooperatives	4,918	6.7%	3,141	7.5%	8,059	7.0%
Apartments	-	0.0%	26,204	62.5%	26,204	22.7%
Manufactured Housing	5,678	7.8%	1,512	3.6%	7,190	6.2%
Total	73,258	100.0%	41,956	100.0%	115,215	100.0%

Source: 2011 American Housing Survey

Through time, there have been some changes in that ratio, but since the 1980s, it has remained relatively constant. Gradually, however, the United States is getting denser as it urbanizes.

Figure 10.5

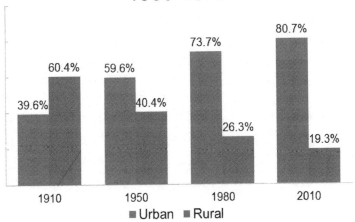

Urban & Rural Population
United States
1900-2010

80.7%

73.7%

60.4%   59.6%

39.6%   40.4%

26.3%

19.3%

1910   1950   1980   2010

■ Urban ■ Rural

Virtually all the growth in the nation for the past two decades has been
urban in nature, and that inevitably means higher-density housing. Most of
those higher-density urban communities are in the fourteen fast-growing
states plus the surviving metropolitan areas.

Higher density is good, because it is environmentally sound and makes for
real neighborhoods. Spreading our housing out over the outlands with
suburban-type lots may look good on paper and has served its purpose
since the end of World War II, when the first Levittowns were built. But
we are in a new age where we must consider the environmental aspects of
housing as well as the sociology of demographics and the need for
"community."

Just the move from a single-family community with 7,500-square-foot lots
built out at four units per acre consumes enormous amounts of
infrastructure compared to townhomes built out at a modest fifteen units
per acre. Imagine the reduction in the amount of curb and gutter, asphalt,
utility lines, and servicing.

Think of as something as simple as postal service. Think of the time it takes to stop at each home and deposit the mail in individual mailboxes as opposed to having a block of postal boxes at the entry to an attached-home project.

The USPS is going broke (is broke). Imagine how much deeper in debt it would be if its service was all to single-family homes. It's bad enough that Congress will not allow it to discontinue Saturday service or buy new vehicles, but even worse is the thought that postal service would be almost entirely a world of individual mailboxes.

As it is, most of our post offices will wind up being integrated into Staples/Office Depot and possibly FedEx and UPS outlets. In fact, if it weren't for the pigheaded Congress, many of the changes I suggest here would long have been instituted. But that's a different story for another time.

It is a given that everyone does not want to live in a downtown high-rise, but tomorrow's urban housing world will consist of more townhomes and low-rise condominiums, very often clustered in villages within master-planned communities with retail and other common-core services within walking distance.

This picture of tomorrow is, in fact, taking shape all over the United States, but particularly in the fast-growing states and the survivor metropolitan areas.

In the same vein, new for-sale attached housing has less square footage. Conversely, for decades, the average single-family home has increased in size. In 1980, the average new home was 1,670 square feet in a metropolitan area, but it has gradually increased to 2,203 square feet, up almost a third.

Figure 10.6

Average Square Footage Single Family Homes United States 1980-2010		
Year	Inside Metropolitan Areas	Outside Metropolitan Areas
1980	1,670	1,450
1990	1,985	1,630
2000	2,121	1,824
2010	2,203	1,877
Change 1980-2010	533	427
% increase	31.9%	29.4%

Simultaneously, the average number of persons per household has shrunk. Therefore, the square footage per person has expanded dramatically.

Figure 10.7

Average Household Size United States 1900-2010	
Year	Persons Per HH
1900	4.60
1950	3.38
1980	2.75
2010	2.59

Now we are seeing a reversal of that trend as urban construction expands. The other trend is that attached projects tend to have fewer units in them than do single-family projects. Historically, the major national homebuilders have often produced thousands of single-family units in their suburban communities. Now, we see master-planned communities with a mix of product, but most often, there are fewer than two hundred units in each project. This gives more of a sense of community than does living in an endless blob of near-identical stucco-clad subdivisions.

I should also mention the conservation benefits of attached living for the individual homeowner. The savings in the use of water, gas, and electric is rather substantial. Having units attached is a major utility savings because two walls in each unit are common. It's basically like having double insulation.

I am not suggesting that everybody in the United States will want to live in a townhome or a vertical condominium, but it is the trend, and it is certainly "smart" growth.

Let's look now at the composition of households in the United States, and particularly in the fourteen fast-growing states. Theoretically, at least, the supply of housing should mirror the composition of the housing market. Thus, if every household had a mom and dad and two kids, my projections would be dramatically different from what I will show you now.

The *Leave It to Beaver* days are long behind us, and the nation's demographics are changing. Here is a snapshot of household composition since 1900.

In 1990, only 20 percent of households contained only one or two members. In the 2010 census, the percentage had tripled. And the number of households with five or more has declined from almost half to less than 10 percent.

Figure 10.8

Households by Size United States 1900-2010				
	% of Households			
No. Persons	1900	1950	1980	2010
1-Person	5.1%	9.3%	22.7%	27.4%
2-Person	15.2%	28.1%	31.3%	33.9%
3-Person	17.8%	22.8%	17.4%	15.7%
4-Person	17.2%	18.4%	15.4%	13.4%
5 or Persons	44.7%	21.4%	13.2%	9.6%
Total	100.0%	100.0%	100.0%	100.0%
1 & 2 Person HHs	20.3%	37.4%	54.0%	61.3%

The composition of married households has changed, too. Now, over half of married couples have no kids under age eighteen living at home, down from 43 percent in 1970. And the number of married couples with three or more kids has dropped by half in that time frame.

Figure 10.9

Household Composition of Families United States 1970-2010		
Category	1970	2010
No kids	42.9%	52.0%
1 kid	18.2%	20.0%
2 kid	18.0%	18.0%
3 or More	20.8%	10.0%
Total	100.0%	100.0%

The change in demographics has been a function of five factors:

- Later marriages
- More years in school
- Fewer and later children
- Major decline in teen birth rates
- Dramatic, disproportionate decline of children added to Hispanic and black households

Perhaps the most important factor in projecting the demand for housing is the age that folks get married and have kids. That is certainly the predominant demand factor in housing sales.

In 1970, half of millennial Americans (those aged eighteen to thirty-four) were married with kids. Today, that percentage has dropped by more than half, with only 20 percent of millennials married with kids.

Figure 10.10

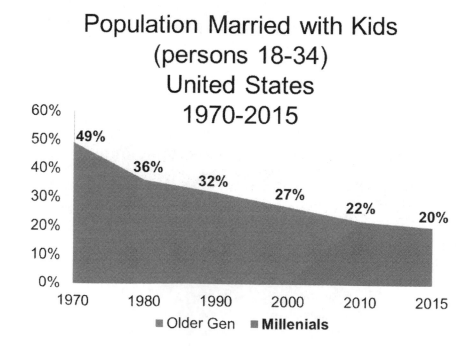

Perhaps even more interesting is the fact that despite the economic recovery, young millennials are opting to live at home with their parents. They are in no hurry to make commitments to marry and have kids.

Figure 10.11

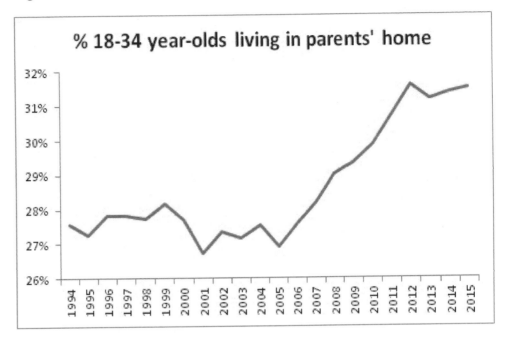

All of these factors are key in the demand for housing.

Production of Housing

The production of housing in the United States rarely relates to demand. Instead, it relates to the availability of construction funds, the appetite of pension funds, and, very often, the supply of shovel-ready dirt.

As a result, there is rarely a period of level production or a production that relates to the formation of households or the marriage rate or the aging of the population.

Figure 10.12

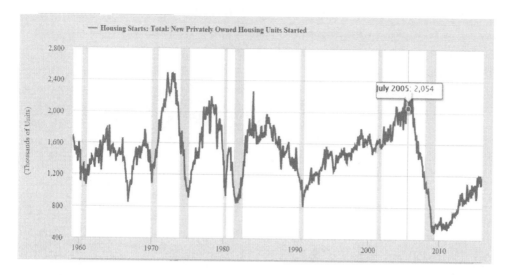

On balance, our nation requires the production of 1.4 to 1.6 million new housing units each year, on average. This number relates to both the formation of new households and the replacement of obsolete housing.

We typically form more than a million households each year in good times, so we are perpetually short of new housing—but most particularly short in those states that account for most of the new household formations (those fourteen now-famous states). We currently are in an interesting period of our history where we are forming many households in those glorious states but producing far fewer housing units than are required to accommodate the new households.

The situation is worse on the West Coast, where environmentalists mandate a perpetual shortage of housing, but it is also evident in many communities in states that have an abundance of land—but that land is typically far removed from jobs in the urban core.

Most prominent of these areas is Phoenix, where the proliferation of housing is an hour or so away from the job core and there is no public transit in sight (well, almost none). The same is true in Orlando, Austin, and the Washington, DC metro. In the DC metro, people travel from as far as Richmond, Virginia to their jobs. At least DC has a wonderful transit system. Not so for the other metros.

The irony of the situation is that the areas with the best jobs have the greatest shortage of rationally priced housing in accessible areas. Excellent examples of this are Seattle, the San Francisco Bay Area, San Jose, San Diego, and, of course, Los Angeles.

California will probably gain 350,000 to 400,000 jobs in each of the next few years (as it has in the past few), but housing production will be in the 100,000 range, and most of that an hour or so away from the employment centers. Not a happy situation.

Unfortunately, this is **not** a fixable problem—at least not in my lifetime. And I intend to live a while longer.

Perhaps I should leave this chapter on a happy note. If you can afford to buy a home today, do it. And if you can afford to buy your children or grandchildren a home, do it. A house remains an exceptionally good annuity, particularly in the fourteen super states.

Conclusion: In every consumer industry in the United States except housing, there is a balance of demand and supply. In the housing industry, particularly in fast-growing areas, there appears to be a concerted effort to have a perpetual imbalance of supply and demand. That is a cruel and inhuman thing, and it need not be that way.

Chapter 11: Apartment Dwellers and Investors

90% of all millionaires became so through owning real estate.

—Andrew Carnegie

This chapter has two subjects: the demographics of renters and investing in apartments.

First, let's take a look at the demographic characteristics of renters and owners and draw a picture of America's renting households.

The Haves and the Have-Nots

In the United States, it is generally acknowledged that those who own homes are the haves, and those who rent are the have-nots. From a net-worth perspective, that is a truism, as most personal net worth is the equity in one's home. And, obviously, a renter has no such equity accumulation.

That said, there are more than a hundred million renters in this nation, almost one-third of the population.

From a trend standpoint, that two-thirds owner, one-third renter ratio has been stable since the 1960s. Based on my reading of the tea leaves, the ratio should remain at the current ratio for several more decades.

The exact ratio, however varies from state to state. In the upper Midwest, many of the states can boast ownership ratios of 75/25, with most of the Midwest in the 65 to 70 percent ownership mode. At the other end of the scale is California, where only 55 percent own and 45 percent rent. That statistic, too, has been stable for decades.

Figure 11.1

	% Own	% Rent
Owner and Renter Occupancy Selected States 2010 Census		
High Owner Occupancy States		
Iowa	72.1%	27.9%
Michigan	72.1%	27.9%
Minnesota	73.0%	27.0%
Utah	70.0%	30.0%
Low Owner Occupancy States		
California	55.9%	44.1%
New York	53.3%	46.7%
District of Columbia	42.0%	58.0%
Hawaii	57.7%	42.3%
Nevada	58.8%	41.2%

Figure 11.2

	Owners		Renters		Total
Owner Renter Tenure United States 1970-2010					
Year	No.	%	No.	%	
1970	40,834,000	64%	22,806,000	36%	63,640,000
1990	60,248,000	64%	33,976,000	36%	94,224,000
2010	75,982,306	65%	40,733,986	35%	116,716,292

During the most recent Bush administration, there was a massive push to increase home ownership. It was a great academic exercise. The thesis was, make it real easy for just about anybody to qualify for a home—with or without a down payment and with or without a verifiable income—and watch home ownership soar. Also, the lender, when borrowers swore they were going to occupy the new home (but already had one), was expected to sort of close its eyes and ears and let the money flow.

Well, we know how that exercise turned out. Yes, for a very few short years, home ownership soared. And then reality set in. And now, several years later, we are back to the two-thirds, one-third ratio. We proved that not everybody was in a position to be a homeowner. There's a certain balance that works in the United States, and disturbing it leads to substantial instability.

This is not to say that every red-blooded American shouldn't have a goal of home ownership—only that there should be a meaningful relationship between financial situation and home ownership.

The Renters

Who are the renters? First, they can be segmented into two categories: temporary and permanent.

Temporary Renters

Temporary renters themselves fall into three categories: not quite ready to buy, change of life conditions, and geographic relocation.

The not quite ready to buy are folks who will buy a home at some point in their lives. The vast majority in this category are under age thirty-five. They may be single or married, and home ownership is something on the horizon, very often when a first child is on the way. (As I noted in an earlier chapter, folks are getting married later and having children later.)

A second category of temporary renter is of those who have owned but have undergone a change in life condition. Very often, the change relates to divorce, job loss, or change in financial condition. It can also be a change of geographic location, where someone has not yet settled in the new locale.

Divorce is a great generator of demand for apartments. More than 90 percent of Americans marry once; 50 percent marry twice, and 15 percent marry three times.

Renters for Life

Renters for life tend to fall into three dominant categories as well: low-income households, households in very expensive metropolitan areas, and those who opt to rent.

The low-income households, more often than not, tend to be blue-collar workers, very often with less than high-school educations. They are often in subsidized housing or receive government housing subsidies. A substantial portion of this category are self-supporting single moms with minimal opportunity to move ahead.

A second category are those who live in obnoxiously high-cost locales like New York City; Boston; the Washington, DC metropolitan area; or almost anywhere in the coastal regions of California. The price of housing for sale in those areas is highly prohibitive for those who are not dual-income, college-educated households.

And finally, there are folks who just do not want to own a home or assume the responsibility of home ownership. They are content being renters, even if they can afford to buy.

Renters and Owners Compared

The three most obvious differentials between renters and owners are age, education, and income.

The age of more than one-third of renters is under thirty-five, compared to 10 percent of owners. At the other end of the scale, 29 percent of owners are over age sixty-five, compared to 14 percent of the renters. Generally speaking, the older you get, the more likely it is that you own your home.

Figure 11.3

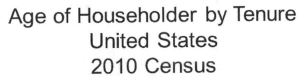

Age of Householder by Tenure
United States
2010 Census

In a similar vein, the higher one's level of education, the more likely one is to own a home. Only 8.8 percent of owners have less than a high-school diploma, compared to twice that for renters. Two-thirds of those with a college education own a home compared to 58 percent of those who rent.

Figure 11.4

Comparison of Education Owners and Renters United States 2010 Census		
Level of Education	Owner-Occupied	Renter-Occupied
Less than high school graduate	8.8%	15.9%
High school graduate	24.6%	26.4%
Some college or associate's degree	30.3%	33.1%
Bachelors degree or high	36.3%	24.6%
Total	100.0%	100.0%

Education, as might be expected, directly relates to household income. Almost 40 percent of renters have household incomes under $25,000, compared to 15 percent of owners. Only 17 percent of renters have household incomes over $75,000, compared to almost half of owners. One-fifth of renters have housing subsidies.

The median income of renters is $33,000, and it is twice that for owners. Not unexpected.

Figure 11.5

Household Income Owners and Renters United States		
Income	Owners	Renters
Under $25,000	15.0%	39%
$25,000-49,999	21.4%	28%
$50,000-74,999	19.2%	16%
$75,000+	44.4%	17%
Total	100.0%	100%
Median	$ 66,828	$ 32,831
Source: 2013 American Community Survey		

Looking at the demography over the next decade, the Joint Center for Housing Studies at Harvard has projected that single people will account for almost half of renter-household growth over the coming decade. There are a lot of folks who just want to live alone.

Figure 11.6

Projections of Renter Household Growth
United States
2010-2020

Household Composition	%
Singles	
Single Person	44.0%
Single Parent	9.0%
Total Single	**53.0%**
Marrieds	
Marrieds without children	17.8%
Married with Children	13.0%
Total Married	**30.8%**
Other Household Types	**16.2%**
Total	100.0%
Source: Harvard Joint Center for Housing Studies	

The projected increase in single-person households during the next ten years is a major increase from levels of the past thirty years. Since 1980, the percent of one-person households has been stable at 36 percent.

Figure 11.7

1-Person Occupied Rental Units United States 1960-2010	
Year	%
1960	20.7%
1970	27.2%
1980	36.0%
1990	35.2%
2000	36.5%
2010	36.2%

The major increase from 1960 to 1980 coincides with the major increase in women in the workforce and the trends toward later marriages.

A Picture of the Rental-Housing Inventory

Almost one-third of our rental-housing inventory consists of single-family detached homes. Half of the rental stock is in projects with nineteen units or less. Only 8.8 percent of rental units are in projects with more than fifty units, and, as might be anticipated, two-thirds of those fifty-plus-unit projects are in urban areas.

Figure 11.8

Structure Type Rental Housing Inventory 2010 Census		
Unit Type	No. Units (000)	%
Single Family Detached	11,714.0	29.1%
Duplex/Fourplex	10,353.0	25.7%
5-19 Units	9,884.0	24.6%
20-49 Units	3,394.0	8.4%
50+ Units	3,534.0	8.8%
Mobile Homes	1,340.0	3.3%
Total	40,219.0	100.0%

Source: American Housing Survey

The rental-housing stock is getting progressively older each year. One quarter of it was built prior to 1950. Only 19 percent of it has been built since 1990.

The median age of a rental unit in the United States is thirty-eight years. As you move from east to west, the rental inventory gets younger. In the east, the median age of a rental unit is fifty-eight, and in the west, thirty-five. But that should come as no surprise.

Figure 11.9

Age of Structure Rental Housing Inventory 2010 Census		
Year Built	No. Units	%
Pre-1950	9,665	24.0%
1950-1970	8,493	21.1%
1970-1990	14,281	35.5%
1990-2010	7,779	19.3%
Total	40,218	100.0%

The Cost of Building New Apartment Units

The key to satisfying rental-housing demand is developing a mix of A- and B-quality projects. A-quality projects are self-explanatory. B-quality projects are those that are affordable by the masses. Rents in this category vary significantly by geography.

In most states, developers are encouraged to build B projects (not subsidized, but market rate). In other states (like the beloved California), cities make it very difficult, if not impossible, to build B projects.

In California near the coast, very often, the exactions placed on the developer often are in the $40,000–$80,000 range—**per unit**. In addition, zoning restrictions, overreaching parking requirements, and other interferences with the development process, along with unusually long processing time and, often, litigation by community-planning groups, means that it is rarely possible to build apartments to rent for less than $2.50 per square foot per month.

Using simple math, a one-thousand-square-foot, two-bedroom apartment would rent for $2,500, not including utilities. This rent level means it is an "A" apartment.

To achieve A rents, it is necessary to include all the bells and whistles in the unit, including washer and dryer, stone countertops, upscale appliances and fixtures, and even high-quality architecture. These inclusions also serve to drive up the rents, but then again, developers have no choice if they want to obtain A rents. The $2.50 per square foot is chicken feed compared to rents in upscale neighborhoods or, often, in downtown areas. On the West Coast, rents for A-quality projects are most often in the $3–$4-per-square-foot range.

Supply-and-Demand Issues

For the most part, the heaviest demand is for B units in expensive areas. The reality is that in areas that are not growing, the demand for new units is minimal. Therefore, the overwhelming shortage of new B units is in the fourteen fast-growing states, but most particularly in states like Washington and California that have obnoxiously high land prices and government exactions.

In those states, if you can afford a B apartment unit, you are probably living in an apartment project that is thirty or forty years old and in a mediocre neighborhood. And you are probably doubling up—or tripling up. Or you are just living with Mom and Dad.

Not to be a negativist, but it is proving impossible to provide B-quality rentals in states like those on the West Coast because the politics are clearly anti-development.

Owning Apartments

Owning apartments is a good thing, particularly in states that are growing. If a state has a stagnant population, the odds of an apartment project increasing in value is minimal, as is the possibility of raising rents. Because it is difficult to raise rents in these stagnant markets, there is little incentive to renovate the project, so the owner winds up with an aging, substandard project and, as a result, rents to substandard tenants.

I'm reminded of a prisoner who complained that the jails had substandard living conditions. The guard reminded him that the prisoners, as well, were substandard.

Perhaps the best opportunities to make obscene profits in the apartment world is remodeling older units in cherished locations. I see this going on all over the nation in metropolitan areas like Boston, Washington, and the entire West Coast. Note that in communities with rent control, little renovation takes place.

When an economy is ebullient, there is the strong possibility of well-located apartment projects being sold to condominium converters. Inevitably, they are willing to pay more than apartment projects typically sell for.

On balance, apartment ownership is very often the basis for rising net worth and enviable estates.

> **Conclusion: Rental housing shelters one-third of all Americans. America is one of few nations in the world that has market-rate apartment complexes. They are unique economic entities that must be maintained and renovated to accommodate those millions who can't or don't want to be in an ownership position.**

Chapter 12: The Whole New World of Retailing and Office Space

Business opportunities are like buses, there is always another one coming.

—Richard Branson

This chapter will capture the highs and lows of the commercial-property markets, not from a traditional real-estate standpoint, but from a demographic standpoint. In other words, demographics will determine the future of the commercial markets, particularly in **retail** and **office**.

As an overall trend, there has been an enormous shift in the composition of tenants throughout the entire retail spectrum as well as an explosion of new retail and service outlets. Perhaps the most remarkable trend is the change in composition of neighborhood centers and strip malls from purveyors of goods to purveyors of services—and the myriad of new services being offered.

Over the past twenty years, we have seen the remarkable expansion of services that people now demand. Included are gyms, massage therapy, nail salons, waxing salons, blow-drying and haircut salons, financial planning, FedEx and UPS outlets, law firms, tax-preparation firms, dentists, car rentals, specialty foods and fast foods, electronics (AT&T, Verizon), beauty supplies, stock brokerage, game shops (like GameStop), and martial-arts studios. And, within each category, numerous national chains have developed to serve these consumer needs.

Even the dining opportunities have exploded over the last twenty years: in my neighborhood, it is possible to dine on sushi, Thai, Vietnamese, Italian, Indian, Korean, Chinese, and Greek food as well as bagels and submarines, and to pig out at the ubiquitous Mexican eateries. This, in addition to the myriad of national fast-food chains.

Even regional centers are seeing the addition of retail outlets that would not have been the norm a quarter century ago. Such chains as Crate and Barrel and Pottery Barn, not to mention Tesla and PIRCH outlets, are now part of the equation for regional-center success.

Retail Space

It is rather obvious to anyone who has watched a six-year-old operate a drone that the delivery of retail goods, and maybe services, will be changing dramatically over the next quarter century.

Traditionally, retailing is in four tranches: regional centers, neighborhood centers (with grocery stores), strip centers, and stand alones (i.e., the Walmarts of the world).

Regional Centers

They are, by and large, not doing well if they are in nongrowing areas, and not well cared for. Many are obsolete and will be razed in the next quarter century. The hundred-year era of department stores is on the wane, as I am certain you have noticed with the disappearance of numerous Sears, Macy's, Robinsons-May, Hecht's, and JCPenney stores. It is apparent that the anchors are sinking. But that's what anchors do, very often.

Many of the regional centers were built a half century ago and are just plain stale. And many of them are in communities that are equally stale and moving from middle-class to lower-middle-class status.

The role of the regional center is entertainment—and if it fails to entertain, it fails. Seniors using regional centers for their morning walkathons doesn't relate to the production of $400-plus-per-square-foot sales that centers need to survive. The modern centers that have learned how to entertain their clienteles will survive, particularly those in upscale areas where the myriad of new women's fashion emporiums prevail. Without women, regional centers wouldn't exist.

Outlet Mall

A subset of the regional center is the outlet mall, a gathering of past-season (or cheaper, direct-to-outlet) goods from most of the major traditional retailers like Coach, Gucci, and so many other upscale, women-oriented stories. The outlet mall appears to prosper most in tourism-oriented metropolitan areas. Most are more than a hundred thousand square feet, with a hundred or more outlet stores.

Stand Alones

Taking the place of the regional center, for the most part, is the stand-alone, "big-box" retailer—like Walmart, Costco, Home Depot, Lowe's, and Target. With sales very often in excess of $1,000 per square foot, these megastores provide not only wonderful bargains, but, in the cases of Walmart, Sam's Club, Target, and Costco, for instance, they also provide food and beverages, carving away some business from the traditional neighborhood grocer.

More recently, these stand alones are becoming less stand alone, acting as anchors of their own, surrounding themselves with the traditional in-line retail and service providers.

It is also obvious that there are too many stand alones, particularly in the case of limited-product outlets. Thus, in the recent recession, we saw the disappearance of Circuit City and Mervyn's, the Sears purchase of Kmart, and the mergers of several chains that supply pet food, hardware, and office supplies.

The Neighborhood Center

The neighborhood center is the traditional center with a supermarket anchor, usually a drugstore, and then a group of mom-and-pop goods-and-services providers.

Supermarkets operate on a very thin profit margin (and always have) and very clearly are struggling to survive. They have worked diligently to provide an ever-widening range of goods and services, including alcoholic-beverage sections, delis, bakeries, bank branches, dry cleaners, and copy shops. Soon they will join drugstores in providing medical services.

Still, most areas are overstored. Perhaps the most disheartening examples are Phoenix and Las Vegas, where during the recent recession, literally dozens of centers saw their anchors vacate, leaving the in-line stores hanging out to dry.

Very often, the anchor store was replaced by a Goodwill outlet, a church, or a school, none of which provided the traffic necessary to draw sufficient business to the in-line stores, so many of them folded as well.

So, in the coming years, we will see fewer and fewer of these neighborhood centers being built, except in new, master-planned communities where new homes will provide the appropriate demand.

Another interesting trend is that in many of the larger neighborhood centers, there is a competing specialty-food outlet like Trader Joe's or a drug chain like CVS or Walgreen's, which also carry a limited selection of food items. Of course, many of the supermarkets also have drugstores within them, so it is tit-for-tat.

Last, particularly for those who live on the West Coast, is the explosion of supermarket-size ethnic-food chains to serve the Hispanic and Asian markets. Such chains as 99 Ranch (Asian) and Northgate (Hispanic) provide a broad range of food and beverages for these enormous ethnic patronages.

The Strip Center

Somewhat like cockroaches, strip centers will be the last surviving form of retailing. These provide goods and services that don't lend themselves well to drone delivery. They tend to be service oriented. It's tough to get a haircut or your nails polished on Amazon (at least at the moment).

And there is, of course, the ubiquitous Starbucks, everybody's new pub, office, and meeting place. Gradually, as it adds wine and beer to its menus, Starbucks will, in fact, become the British pub that we sorely need in this country—without the steak-and-kidney pie, thankfully.

Free Delivery and Endless Choices

I am most anxious to see the changes in the next few years in goods-delivery systems. I find the ability to receive same-day delivery from Amazon and its minions remarkable. Combining UPS, FedEx, USPS, and drones feeds Americans' needs for instant gratification, along with the ability to return things that don't meet one's fancy.

©Henrique Boney

We know that 15 percent of all goods ordered online is returned. The ability to return goods without leaving your home is an enormous benefit. New businesses are now being established to handle the returns for the Amazons of the world. Few returns actually go back on the shelf for resale.

Better yet, the ability to shop on an Amazon and have an amazingly broad range of products and spirited pricing competition, along with the ability to see honest and often detailed ratings on the product lines, puts the consumer in the driver's seat. It is rather remarkable, I think. Or, of course, if you need something from a local merchant that doesn't deliver, you can always call Uber to pick it up for you.

We Americans are definitely being spoiled rotten in this wonderful new world of retailing that we now live in. And how could we live without Google?

Overall Supply and Demand

Traditionally, research indicates that the demand for retail space is equivalent to fifteen or twenty square feet per capita. Currently, there are twelve billion square feet of retail space in the United States, which means a per capita of fifty-four square feet.

Generally speaking, then, we are wildly overretailed, and therefore we will continue to see the razing of old shopping centers and precious few new ones being built. The problem of too much retailing is particularly acute in metros that have stagnant or declining population and/or a population base that does not have sufficient disposable income to support the existing retail space.

On the Way Up — and On the Way Down

Retail business has a way of reflecting the times and the needs and wants of the American consumer. Many of us remember Mervyn's, Circuit City, OfficeMax (bought by Office Depot), and a host of other chains that have disappeared in recent years. Here are a few that are on the way up and a few that are on the way down:

Figure 12.1

Number of Stores Selected Retailers 2000 and 2015				
	No. Stores			
Direction	2000	2015	Change	% Change
On the Way Up				
Target	977	1,805	828	84.7%
Walmart	1,985	5,310	3,325	167.5%
Home Depot	1,134	2,269	1,135	100.1%
On the Way Down				
Sears	2,063	709	(1,354)	-65.6%
J.C. Penneys	1,143	1,020	(123)	-10.8%
Toys R Us	1,086	872	(214)	-19.7%

Source: K-1 Securities and Exchange Commission

The Mini Hospital

The greatest change in retailing in the years to come will be the incorporation of medical facilities in chain stores. Currently, almost all the drugstore chains are operating clinics, most in joint ventures with local hospitals and universities. Before long, all the department stores, big-box stores, and prominent retailers will have clinics on site.

This is a brilliant idea for two reasons: first, it offers employees a very reasonably priced alternative to an emergency room, and they can care for their ills before they get serious. Second, it will dramatically reduce the hospitals' cost of serving the public.

Together, these two benefits will help drive down the overall cost of medicine in this nation. As is well known, we spend 17 percent of our gross product on medical care, almost twice that of the other industrialized nations—and yet, there is no indication of our population being healthier. (Of course, our obesity and torpor do have a great deal to do with our obscene medical costs.)

Office Space

Office space is going through almost as much of a revolution as retailing. The primary culprits in this revolution are the laptop computer and the cell phone.

A few years ago, one of our apartment-development clients asked us to determine the demand for work-live apartment units. We gathered data from several dozen management firms in San Diego. In total, our database contained about fifty thousand apartment units. We asked the resident managers to count the cars in the lot at 10:00 in the morning.

We had interesting findings: the higher the quality and rental rate of the apartment, the higher the percentage of cars in the lot at ten in the morning. In other words, the lower-income apartment dwellers were still going to work in the traditional manner, but the upper-income residents were working at home, at least part of the time.

Thus, the traditional office worker, now working part time at home, did not need the traditional office on a full-time basis. Further, in the past, a myriad of traditional office tenants used to spend a good part of their days outside the office visiting clients, but these folks still had formal offices when they came in from the field. That situation is rapidly changing. A quarter century ago, the norm was four hundred square feet per employee. Today, that ratio has fallen to 150 to 200 square feet per and is moving down rapidly.

Accounting firms, for instance, were the first to go to the "hoteling" concept, where offices or cubicles were not individually designated but open to whomever needed them. The accountant could come into the office, plug in his or her laptop, recharge the cell phone, and be off and running.

Law firms, which once had huge libraries, found them unnecessary with the advent of firms like Thomson Reuters, which has eight thousand attorneys searching case law and new decisions. Any law firm can subscribe to its services, and even a one-person law firm can have research capabilities that were once available only to the largest firms. This also means that there is no longer a need for a host of young law graduates to search through libraries, so law firms can do with far fewer employees than in the past.

As an ancillary trend, we find that the traditional downtown space users are moving at least part of their staffs to suburban locations, which are typically less expensive and very often where their employees live anyway.

The proliferation of high-end suburban office space is creating new mini towns in many areas. In the San Francisco Bay Area, places like Oyster Point and Redwood City are bulging with firms that need to be close to San Francisco but don't want to pay the stiff tariff that is the hallmark of San Francisco office space.

At the same time, the enormous amount of loose capital in the Bay Area allows many of these techie firms to acquire space in the city or to build their own spaces. Salesforce.com is going to occupy almost 800,000 square feet in a high-rise in downtown San Francisco next to a major transit center.

Similarly, in Los Angeles, Century City is a major outpost for firms who opt not to be in downtown Los Angeles. In San Diego, Carmel Valley plays a similar role.

And, of course, the rise of Brooklyn as an alternative to Manhattan is legendary. Brooklyn now has fifty million square feet of office space—not quite rivaling Manhattan's four hundred million, but a good start nonetheless.

Often taking the place of the traditional tenants is the newly created category of techies. Downtowns, in particular, are encouraging creators of software and other engineering marvels to move to city cores. As employees of these firms tend to be single millennials, they want to be where they can live, work, and party without the need for a car.

Within the office itself, there is a definite trend toward the open-office concept. In the old days (ten years ago), it was still a mark of achievement to have a private office with a window. And the larger the window, the higher the level of achievement. Today, with the open-office environment, the CEO may be sitting in the middle of the office space without a window or a door.

This trend also means that techies may not be in an office building at all. They may in an open office in a renovated industrial building with high ceilings and funky surroundings.

Last, we see the rise of the rent-an-office industry. Here, you can rent an office by the hour or day or month. And, as your firm grows, it can just add offices. They are furnished and ready to go, with conference rooms, secretarial assistance, and copy rooms built in. And often, they are luxurious.

The largest chain of furnished offices is Regus, with three thousand locations in nine hundred cities in 120 countries worldwide. For traveling folks, it's a real blessing. In every city you visit, you get the same office. There are six Regus offices in mid-Manhattan alone.

A growing number of furnished-office providers are aimed at the techies and others who collaborate with like-minded folk. In San Diego, entrepreneur Dennis Cruzan has converted a 175,000-square-foot former flower-trade center into a multitenant office setting called MAKE. It will have a fitness center and a view of the ocean.

Pointedly, the demand for downtown office space in most metropolitan areas is on the wane or stable at best. The era of massive office construction in downtown areas is passé, except in a very few places like Manhattan and the Loop in Chicago.

Do note, however, that for the most part, the nation's office inventory is showing its age, and there are many national firms that want new, class A office space in major metropolitan areas.

In addition, whereas government has traditionally been centered in downtown areas, it, too, is spreading out into suburban campuses throughout the nation, further weakening the downtown space markets.

Some downtowns are coming back to life. Certainly, that is true in Los Angeles, which has a hundred residential and commercial projects in the pipeline. San Francisco, which had virtually no construction underway for years, now has sixty-three thousand housing units under construction. There appears to be a crane on every block in the midcity area and south of Market.

Conclusion: The world of retailing and office space is getting increasingly more exciting as yesterday fades into history and expectations of the consumer grow exponentially. Choice is an integral part of what makes America great.

Chapter 13: The Remarkable Story of Personal Net Worth

Money makes the world go around
The world go around
A mark, a yen, a buck, or a pound
A buck or a pound
Is all that makes the world go around,
That clinking clanking sound
Can make the world go 'round.

—Kander and Ebb, from **Cabaret**

I am an optimist at heart, but there is economic weight behind my optimism, particularly as it concerns the United States.

I want to tell you the real reason that the States will have core financial strength over the next quarter century (and probably longer). It has to do with demography. Over the next twenty-five years, the post-World War II generation will pass on. **It is the first generation in world history to have had personal net worth. That concept didn't exist seventy-five years ago except for a handful of the elite, who were mostly based in Manhattan.**

In that much-heralded baby boomer generation, we not only had enormous heroism and great personal strength, we also had the beginning of social security, life insurance, pension funds, urban home ownership, and savings accounts. That generation remembered the Depression. Of this group, 80 percent owned homes, and few had mortgages. It also believed in delayed gratification—all to the benefit of its heirs. This was manna from the Met.

It is that "greatest generation" that is in the process of leaving more than $40 trillion to its sons and daughters and grandchildren (and some charities).

The heirs of that generation will fuel enormous consumer spending, provide college tuition, buy nice homes and vacation homes and leather-outfitted cars and international vacations and keep Nordstrom and Patagonia in business. And the same phenomenon will also provide confidence in the economy.

Think of how many people you know in the forty-to-sixty-year-old range who are living better than they ever have. And you can surmise that it's not from job promotions.

Let's look at these people.

Household Income

Back in 1900, it took almost half our population to provide food from the farm for our table. Now it's 3 percent.

In terms of the nation's cumulative **household income** (and therefore the ability to spend), it has risen exponentially, thanks to a combination of a change in the number of households, the dramatic increase in two-job households, and rising income. The total number of households has increased 181 percent since 1970, and total household income has increased 250 percent. Europe, eat your heart out.

Figure 13.1

Total Household Income United States 1970-2010			
Year	No. of Households	Mean Income (dollars)	Total Income (dollars)
1970	64,778	$ 49,301	$ 3,193,620,178
1990	94,312	$ 59,505	$ 5,612,035,560
2010	117,538	$ 67,976	$ 7,989,763,088
Change 1970-2010	181%	138%	250%

Home Ownership

Of all Americans, 80 percent over age fifty-five own a home. Better yet, 65 percent of them own their homes with no mortgage. And the 35 percent who do have mortgages have average monthly payments of $750. This is chicken feed.

Figure 13.2

Age Range	Owner-Occupied	Renter - Occupied	Total	% Owner
	Tenure by Age Group			
	United States			
	2014			
Total	116,211,092	41,423,632	157,634,724	74%
55-59	8,753,818	2,867,083	11,620,901	75%
60-64	8,139,061	2,270,292	10,409,353	78%
65-74	11,686,414	2,818,552	14,504,966	81%
75-84	6,701,076	1,757,657	8,458,733	79%
85+	2,452,105	1,119,167	3,571,272	69%
over 55	**37,732,474**	**10,832,751**	**48,565,225**	**78%**
over 65	**20,839,595**	**5,695,376**	**26,534,971**	**79%**

Life Insurance

Life insurance was almost unheard of at the beginning of the twentieth century. In fact, it really wasn't until after World War II that life insurance became a major financial force. In 2013, there was **$20 trillion in life insurance** in force, twice that of 1990.

Figure 13.3

Life Insurance in Force United States 1900-2013		
Year	$Millions	Index
1900	$ 7,573	
1940	$ 151,762	20.0
1990	$ 9,392,597	1,240.3
2000	$ 15,953,267	2,106.6
2013	$ 19,661,518	2,596.3

Source: ACJI tabulations of Natl Assn. of Insurance Commissioners

Social Security

The Social Security Administration started during the Depression, and its Trust Fund grew very slowly until after 1960. From that point, it grew exponentially and now stands at many trillions of dollars. **The Trust Fund has expanded 427 times since 1940.**

And, contrary to popular opinion, it is not running out of money—at least for the next quarter century. (And, as an aside, the problems of Social Security's income stream could be corrected with a few modest changes that I won't discuss here.)

Figure 13.4

Social Security Trust Fund (millions) 1940-2014		
Year	$	Index
1940	$ 2,011	1.0
1960	$ 22,613	11.2
1990	$ 225,277	112.0
2014	$ 859,230	427.3

Source: Social Security Administration

Public and Private Pension Funds

Since 1985, the value of public and private pension funds has **increased seven times**. In 1985, the total was $2.5 billion and is now $17.7 billion. The rise in 401(k) plans has been remarkable. And though public-sector pension obligations are bankrupting many municipalities, for the most part, the majority will survive.

Figure 13.5

Financial Assets Public and Private Pension Funds United States 1975-2015		
Year	$Billions	Index
1975	$ 960	1.00
1995	$ 2,559	2.67
2005	$ 11,376	11.85
2015	$ 17,702	18.44

FRS Statistics Release Z.1, Financial Assets of the U.S.

Household Real Estate

The value of household real estate has **increased fifteen times since 1975**, although it did not increase much since 2005 as the result of the recent recession. The recession aside, there has still been an enormous increase in the value of household real estate (the category excludes commercial real estate).

Figure 13.6

Household Real Estate ($ Billions) United States 1975-2015		
Year	$	Index
1975	$ 1,684	1.00
1995	$ 8,835	5.25
2005	$ 24,139	14.33
2015	$ 24,981	14.83

Source: FRB Z.1 Financial Assets of the US, L117

Household Net Worth

Based on the Federal Reserve Board's calculations, household net worth **has also increased fifteen times since 1975**. The data wasn't available by age category, but it is evident that household net worth has increased exponentially in the past four decades.

Figure 13.7

Household Net Worth United States 1975-2015		
Year	$	Index
1975	$ 5,795	1.00
1995	$ 29,233	5.04
2005	$ 65,789	11.35
2015	$ 85,182	14.70

Source: FRB Z.1 Financial Assets of the US, L117

Who Are the Losers?

There has to be a segment of the population that does not share in the glory that is upon us. That segment is predominantly the single moms with no college education. They will be doomed to scratching out a living with a life of minimum-wage jobs and government assistance.

And, inevitably, the losers include the men without the ability to read plans or instructions or take direction or move up the chain of management. They will continue to suffer. We, as a nation, have not done a very good job of training that sector of the population.

Conclusion: The next quarter century will bring an explosion of changes in positive net worth, spending habits, housing, medicine, electronics, robotics, and telecommunication. You ain't seen nothin' yet!

Here is *The Great Divide*, all summarized in three pages:

1. The industrialized world will continue to add population and jobs, albeit more slowly in Europe but more so in Mexico, India, and China. **The United States will continue to increase its population by three million annually, indefinitely.**

2. 75 percent of the population and job gains in the United States will be in fourteen states. The important metro areas of those states ring the country, from Seattle and around the South and up the East Coast through the DC/Maryland/Virginia area. The Mountain states of Utah and Colorado are included among the growth winners. The states that will win are those that focus on tomorrow's industries.

3. The median age of the industrialized countries of the world is rising. Europe, Japan, Korea, and Russia are leading the aging process. By 2040, most of the industrialized nations will have a median age of fifty or more. The United States remains the youngest of the industrialized nations because of the youth of the Hispanic market.

4. The Hispanic market (native and immigrating) is the salvation of the States. The Hispanic market is the primary reason that the fourteen key states are prospering. The Hispanics provide the entry-level labor necessary for economies in the United States to survive.

5. Every metropolitan area has the same ratio of basic to support jobs (1:2). The addition of one basic job creates two support jobs. (A basic job is one whose source of revenue is predominantly from outside the metropolitan area.) Markets that have declining basic jobs eventually go bankrupt because a preponderance of the jobs remaining are in the public sector.

6. The fast-growing metropolitan areas are those that have fostered tomorrow's industries, particularly electronics, information, science, biotech, and telecommunications and/or have become

major distribution centers. These areas also have attracted the world's brightest young (and best-paid) professionals.

7. There are a number of survivor metropolitan areas that are not in the fast-growing states. Markets like New York, Chicago, and Boston each have enduring economic characteristics that will allow them to prosper (even if they have lost their manufacturing bases). Most of the survivors are heavy on highly respected educational, health-service, and finance institutions and are headquarter towns.

8. The stagnant metropolitan areas have lost their way. Their basic industries have lost so many jobs in the past quarter century that there is no way they can resurrect those industries or replace them.

9. Home ownership will remain a paramount part of the American DNA. It will remain at its present 67 percent owner to 33 percent renter ratio (which varies somewhat by state and metropolitan area). In the high-priced areas, home ownership could fall below 50 percent as homes become unaffordable, personified by the Bay Area, New York, and Los Angeles metros. New homes will be smaller because of the declining size of households, the rising price of land in the favored metropolitan areas, and the trend toward multifamily housing for sale.

10. In the fast-growing markets, owner-occupied townhomes will become the product of choice (as they always have been in the greater Northeast United States). In the stagnant markets, home ownership will remain high and very cheap, but not cheap enough to entice workforce immigration.

11. Apartments will continue to be attractive for both nonowners and investors. Like homes, rental apartment units will get smaller as more people opt to live alone. Apartment square footage in new projects could shrink by 30 to 40 percent in popular metropolitan areas. Apartment renovation will be the hot investment product over the next quarter century. But our apartment stock is aging. There are thirty million apartment units in the nation, and we only build four hundred to five hundred thousand units annually.

12. The United States is changing rapidly in terms of the demand for office and retail space.